AF886606

COMPLETE FINANCIAL FREEDOM

Strong Trust | Smart Choices

how Christians of wealth cross the chasm of chaos with a true financial steward

Steve A. Swords, CPA
with Benjamin H. Dean, CFP®

ISBN: 0998405906
ISBN: 9780998405902

Printed in the United States of America

DEDICATION

To all our fabulous clients, both current and deceased, to whom we made the claim, “We want to be the last financial advisor you will ever need.” Thank you.

And to some now at home in heaven, who took us seriously, we offer this in your remembrance. God bless you.

CONTENTS

>> PREFACE

STEVE'S STORY

POSITIONED TO SERVE

Whoever wants to become great among you must be your servant
and whoever wants to be first must be your slave.

– MATTHEW 23:11 NIV

The purpose of human life is to serve, and
to show compassion and the will to help others.

– ALBERT SCHWEITZER

Whatever you do in word or deed,
do all in the name of the Lord Jesus....

– COLOSSIANS 3:17

>> I FOUND MYSELF LOOKING UPWARD AND TEARS FLOWING DOWNWARD ...IN THAT DAY I SAID,

"GOD, WHATEVER YOU SHOW ME TO DO, I WILL DO. AS LONG AS I KNOW IT IS YOU, I WILL DO IT!"

>> HE WANTED ME TO...BECOME A "MINISTER" IN THE MARKETPLACE. I UNDERSTOOD THAT ALL CHRISTIANS ARE CALLED TO "MINISTER" BECAUSE ALL ARE CALLED TO "SERVE."

Radical Conversion

I wanted to be a minister. God wanted me to be a steward for people of wealth to preserve the resources of the kingdom and so they could enjoy *complete* financial freedom. Guess who won?

In 1982-1983 my life was spiraling out of control and the path seemed downward to destruction. I never knew that a real relationship with God could help me rise up and be a better man.

I had a 2-month old baby daughter and a 3-year-old son.

I had quit my CPA job with a major public accounting firm.

I had chased a "get rich quick" scheme in multilevel market sales.

I had moved my family across the country to a place 1,500 miles from my nearest relatives.

I was lacking any real parental guidance in my life as my father and mother had divorced a few years earlier and seemed somewhat disinterested in me.

Although somehow always maintaining financial solvency, I was living month to month and feeling exceptionally vulnerable to financial failure.

And someone asked me if Jesus was "the Lord of my life." Seemed like a very odd question given all the other things I was concerned about.

I remember being at a Full Gospel Businessman's Fellowship conference and a man coming up and asking me if Jesus was Lord of my life.

I was 1,500 miles from by brothers and sister and frankly didn't know what he was talking about and I told him so.

"Who is the pilot of your life?" he said.

"Why, I am," I retorted.

That was all about to change.

From the moment I believed in Jesus and asked Him to be Lord of my life, I was changed forever. I didn't know or recognize the changing at first. But I was. I was changing inside. As they say, "I had been lost. But now, I was found. I had been blind, but now, I could see"; or at least for me, I found a path that felt right, and true, and good.

And it gave me a sense that no matter what came my way in life, with Him I would be OK.

Keep in mind, my initial conversion was a bit radical. Not really growing up with any spiritual leadership and discipleship, at 28 years old, I was a dead man walking. Though I had been going regularly to church and even baptized as a child, I did not really "know" Jesus. He was the one who hung on the cross. The idea of Him being the lord-leader of my life was remote at best.

By some divine appointment, I was "born again" and filled with the Holy Spirit all in about one week. Being somewhat stubborn, though I believed in Jesus and asked Him to be Lord, I was not about to have someone "shove" the Holy Spirit on me. But men who love God prayed for me and the hound of heaven knew my address, found me, and fell upon me.

I remember having such an unusual appetite for the Word of God and the truth. I could only imagine that the Holy Spirit was giving me a strong unction to study the Bible. I really needed to know the God who seemed so personal to me; the God of the Bible; not some "made-up god" of men. For me, this unction became a voracious appetite for the truth.

Sometimes I studied six to eight hours a day around my work schedule.

I didn't really understand what I was going through but found a good church and some mentors that helped me grow spiritually.

By that time, we had moved back to my home state of Texas, but not my hometown. We settled in east Texas, remaining about 100 miles from my past. Not that my past was anything abnormal. As a matter of fact, it was so normal it managed to leave out much of the God of the Bible.

I found some men who loved the God I was getting to know, the God and Father of our Lord Jesus Christ. They began to disciple and mentor me in the truth and how to be an effective follower of Jesus.

My wife and I began to see incredible evidence of a loving, all knowing, and all powerful God willing to interfere and affect our lives.

And He wanted a personal relationship with us.

Though often unexplainable, He seemed at times to make Himself knowable in new and fuller ways.

And He loved us and seemed to always want the best for us.

In some of our weakest moments, His Spirit would "show up" to strengthen and encourage us.

Remember, I was no one special except for this enormous appetite for the word of truth which never left me. Then one day I found myself looking upward and tears flowing downward as I sensed what could only have been the strong presence of the Lord Jesus Christ and the living God. In that day I said, "God, whatever you show me to do, I will do. As long as I know it is you, I will do it!" That was the day I knew I was to enter the ministry. I just didn't understand God's version of "ministry."

Over the next few years I joined "a ministry," left "a ministry" and went out "to minister" on short-term foreign mission trips. At first, I joined a ministry part-time as I still had my CPA and financial advisory practice. I was definitely trying to be faithful to go where God would send me. To go to "minister" and then come back to "work." As I like to say, "I had one foot in the ministry and one foot in the marketplace."

I continued this in-depth study of the Bible and even studied Bible history and systematic theology, eventually becoming ordained to "minister." But nothing prepared me for the next clear direction I received from God.

One day as I prayed fervently for release into a greater "ministry," it seemed as though God was telling me something I did not want to hear. My emotions overwhelmed me but I prayed on. The storm in my mind and my emotions seemed to give way to the deep desire to keep my commitment: "Whatever you show me to do, I will do."

Serving the Lord Wherever He Wants

Over the next few weeks, God made it clear in prayer and in His word that "ministry" simply meant "service." He wanted me to serve Him in the marketplace. He wanted me to lift my foot from the "ministry" and become a "minister" in the marketplace. I understood that all Christians are called to "minister" because all are called to "serve."

The biblical word "minister" literally means "serve." Jesus taught, "Whoever wants to become great among you must be your servant, and whoever wants to be first must be your slave (bondservant - lit. household servant)." (Matthew 20:26-27 NIV)

THE SEASON OF TRUE FINANCIAL STEWARDSHIP

My life would never be the same. My success would be in serving others. I was determined to be God's minister wherever I served. During the season of my life that spanned from 1983 to 2016, my service was going to be primarily in financial and investment advisory services.

I wanted to be a minister. God wanted me to become a household servant, a steward, for people of wealth so that they could enjoy *complete* financial freedom.

I founded Swords Wealth Management, LLC to do this work. To a certain extent, the story of Swords Wealth Management, LLC ("SWM") is my story. I would seek to be found a *true financial steward*. And when I prepared for retirement, the new advisors of SWM would need the same objective. After all, I would entrust to them "the stewardship" of all my clients and I would become one of them.

In This Book

In this book the reader will learn my story of developing a practice POSITIONED TO SERVE others while working as unto the Lord. The practice delivers ***the steward's assurance*** and provides clients with *complete* financial freedom.

Learn how I sought someone to join me and eventually take over that practice; someone who could give my family the same assurance and freedom it was delivering to its clients.

You will discover what highly responsible servants should be; men like Ben Dean of SWM. You will discover such true "stewards" can be trusted to manage our financial resources. You will be given the starting point to the TRACK of TRUST in your plans and how to find that faithful person or firm to work your plan. And you will hear about *the bridge* to cross *the chasm of chaos* and reach *complete* financial freedom.

YOU WILL LEARN:

That trust is quantifiable. And we want STRONG TRUST.

That *true financial stewards* are accountable. And we should have clear expectations and experiences that *STRENGTHEN TRUST.*

That financial peace of mind and *complete* financial freedom are obtainable. But we need our servant to deliver on ***the***

steward's assurance to help guide us away from the emotional cliffs and toward the bridge to get there.

Enjoy!

>> CHAPTER 1

TRUE FINANCIAL STEWARDS

FINANCIAL FREEDOM PROVIDERS

Whoever can be trusted with very little can also
be trusted with much, and whoever is dishonest
with very little will also be dishonest with much.
So if you have not been trustworthy in handling worldly wealth,
who will trust you with true riches?
– LUKE 16:10-11 NIV

Who then is the faithful and sensible steward,
whom his master will put in charge of his servants,
to give them their rations at the proper time?
Blessed is that slave whom his master
finds so doing when he comes.
Truly I say to you that he will put him
in charge of all his possessions.
– LUKE 12:42-44

>> *COMPLETE* FINANCIAL FREEDOM WITH ITS FINANCIAL PEACE OF MIND IS AVAILABLE ONLY ON THE OTHER SIDE OF A LARGE AND DEEP CHASM.

>> WHEN A STEWARD SUCCESSFULLY ACKNOWLEDGES AN OWNER'S INDIVIDUAL CONCERNS AND NEEDS, THIS *TRUE FINANCIAL STEWARD* REMAINS ABLE TO RESPOND WELL ON BEHALF OF EACH UNIQUE CLIENT. THEY WILL GAIN AUTHORITY IN THEIR VOICE AND THEIR SERVICE WILL SMELL OF THAT PERFUME OF PEACE.

Steve's Story: The Faithful and Wise Stewards

My wife and I wanted to release all responsibility for our personal wealth management. We wanted *complete* financial freedom. If you are a person of wealth, you should too. FYI: we are persons of wealth if we have accumulated enough resources that to lose 20% would be a significant event in our financial life.

The smart money has known for a long time that the cost of responsible wealth management is minimal compared to the emotional value and time freedom.

Unfortunately, *complete* financial freedom, with its financial peace of mind, is available only on the other side of a large and deep chasm. And *the bridge* across this chasm is not an easy one to take.

I developed the perfect practice to operate as a financial freedom facilitator. We operated as "stewards" on behalf of our clients. In case you're wondering, a "steward" is just a manager. But he is not any ordinary manager.

I ran the practice this way for more than 30 years. Then I turned it over to another *true financial steward* to operate. Now, since I'm semi-retired, I have delegated the responsibility for my personal wealth management to my protégé, Ben Dean, CFP®.

This book is my story of how I went from an advisor training a protégé, to an owner who crossed *the bridge* to *complete* financial freedom. You too can get there.

The Bible refers to an owner who did something very similar to what I did. That owner put a faithful steward "in charge of all his possessions" (Luke 12:42-44). Someone might ask, "Who in their right mind would do such a thing? Entrust all his possessions to another?"

Well, that's exactly what I did. And most of us would readily admit that the financial world is so chaotic that no one can have *complete* freedom from the responsibilities of wealth without doing exactly as this owner in the bible story and I did.

Why is the chasm between wealth responsibilities and releasing those responsibilities to enjoy financial freedom so great? What issues make putting a delegate "in charge" so difficult? Why is it that more people don't experience *complete* freedom from wealth management concerns?

COMPLETE FREEDOM WITH THE STEWARD'S HELP

Let's define financial freedom for people of wealth. Wouldn't it be financial freedom if we could delegate most of our financial and investment affairs to a highly responsible person to handle while knowing all our goals requiring money were being taken care of?

There are many standards set in the Bible for Christians to try to live out. But none is so close to my heart as the parables in the Bible that refer to the *faithful* and *wise* stewards. [Luke 16:10-12; Matthew 24:45-47; Luke 12:45-48]

I founded the practice of Swords Wealth Management, LLC ("SWM") to be financial stewards for family wealth; servants that could truly help clients fully release financial responsibilities for wealth. I wanted my clients to be free from the world of complexities and confusion in financial planning and wealth management; a world of chaos and concerns. I call this *the chasm of chaos*. It is a deep and wide gulf of financial concerns.

This chasm has dangerous cliffs. Despite an advisor being a highly responsible person, clients must still avoid these cliffs. But a *true financial steward* can be great help in this also if the owner will accept help.

The smart money longs for highly responsible stewards to whom to delegate wealth management and who can help them avoid the financial and emotional cliffs for years to come.

HIGHLY RESPONSIBLE STEWARDS: *FINANCIAL FREEDOM* PROVIDERS

We are tired of seeing only self-serving brokers, insurance agents and advisors. There should be a set of criteria in order to determine if someone truly has a heart to serve us, the owners.

Of course, many household owners are *do-it-yourselfer* people. They really don't know how to delegate and release responsibility to others and still be comfortable. Until they do, they will never experience *complete* financial freedom.

One of the reasons that they don't want to delegate and release financial authority is because they truly believe no one will be as responsible for their financial well-being as they would. This is a perfect picture of the chasm between wealth responsibilities and financial freedom.

Lay people consider the responsibilities so broad and the chasm so deep that a bridge of *high faith* is too difficult to take. They consider financial responsibility something that can't be delegated.

But what if the chasm could be crossed? The path to develop *high faith* was reasonable? Are there any other reasons they should delegate as soon as possible?

The answer is "yes."

First, some could permanently damage their financial well-being and put themselves back to working for a living. They stay in denial, knowing they lack the knowledge, skills and experience to manage their own wealth but do so any way. How smart is that?

Second, examine the cost to benefit ratio of hiring a steward. You will probably never go back to do-it-yourself.

Finally, there is great joy in fully releasing the responsibilities of managing wealth. And there are highly responsible financial stewards available. Just consider the advisors of SWM [www.swordswealthmanagement.com].

MY STEWARDSHIP PRACTICE

I share the practice story, which is really my story over the last 33 years, because so many Christians of wealth are lost when it comes to who to trust. And they are confused as to WHAT constitutes good expectations and great service.

It is the story of WHO I became.

I was willing to bear the burden of great expectations and be a financial steward for many households. I wanted to see my clients truly helped to release wealth worries.

Then I trained my replacement and established the principles of the stewardship practice he now manages. I personally tested my replacement as the steward of my personal wealth. Persons of wealth should know these stewardship principles of wealth management and what to expect in a world-class servant.

From my early days years ago to today, the household steward principles have evolved, but never weakened. They are a commitment. For example, now the practice calls themselves *true financial stewards* and *financial freedom providers*. I didn't refer to it that way at first because it seemed confusing to some clients who just wanted simple account management. But between God and me, it was the same thing. The concept sinks deep to the core of helping clients experience *complete* financial freedom.

My mission was not merely to "manage the money" or to manage brokerage accounts like so many investment advisors limit themselves to do. My mission was to serve "the master's house" so to speak. The mission has always been to help the owner to fully release all responsibilities of their wealth management. I knew that for the owner to have *complete* financial freedom, they would have to entrust "all" wealth responsibilities into a true financial steward's care.

To do this, I had to prove myself and the practice worthy of that delegation and encourage them to fully release "their stewardship" to me. Also, and frankly this is the hard part for the steward, I would have to be prepared to bear the burden of care for "all" their wealth.

Sounds almost unrealistic doesn't it? The owner would have to have STRONG TRUST. Who could develop such *high faith* to delegate all their assets? And what advisor would be willing to work like a slave?

But God gave me the grace and began to send me great Christian clients who recognized my heart to serve and my practice as a stewardship. Clients started with little trust and worked up.

I learned both the client and myself had some learning curve in this relationship if we were going to develop STRONG TRUST in each other and they were going to experience financial freedom.

We had to respect the *chasm of chaos*. They had to learn to step away from the cliffs, the personal pitfalls to their peace of mind that had nothing to do with whether I was a good steward. I had to embrace the many "little things" of their unique values and goals and how to speak with my voice of authority to assure them our bridge crossed the chasm of their concerns.

But we both learned the relationship was worth it. Developing this TRACK OF TRUST would give them *complete* financial freedom.

A true steward could be the perfect financial freedom provider under two (2) conditions:

1) If the owner would step away from the cliffs and toward *the bridge*, and
2) If I could live up to the biblical steward standard with knowledge, skill and experience, and do my part in helping them bridge the *chasm of chaos*.

MY STEWARD'S AUTHORITY: FROM LITTLE TO *COMPLETE*

When the Bible refers to the *faithful* and *wise* stewards, it speaks of trustworthiness with "the little things." It implies that IF this manager is found faithful and wise in the "little things" – the testing period responsibilities, particularly in the use of another's "worldly wealth" – the owner should feel able to entrust "all his possessions" to the steward.

Entrusting "all his possessions" sounds like a real stretch of faith for the owner who has never worked with a steward like me or a practice like mine. That owner faces the very real chasm of current events and concerns: not knowing what to do themselves, weak trust in advisors, unclear expectations, the pressure to give in to the "blind faith" appeal of so many salespeople, and many other reasons to worry.

What assures the owner that this "steward" will act any differently? That he or she is trustworthy? That he or she will "be there" in time of need to help them bridge the chaos?

We should not overlook the big "IF" in the biblically inspired owner/steward relationship. Before entrusting "all our possessions," setting big prerequisites is okay. Under scrutiny, this manager must first be found...

- ...faithful or trustworthy (i.e., in things like "proper time," "proper portion," etc)
- ...wise or sensible (i.e., smart choices with insight, etc).

There is a testing season, a trial period, to test the "faithful" and "wise" reality of that delegate. Testing some "little things" in route to *complete* release is normal. It is not what a person says as much as what a person does that shows the integrity behind their service.

Owners should expect their delegate to act with what we call the "steward's authority." The faithful and wise experiences are what become key in ***the steward's authority***. These truly yield financial peace of mind. It only comes with time and through actual experience in financial management.

In my world, trust would begin by helping the owner set clear and reasonable expectations. Then I would prove myself trustworthy with those "little" expectations. With this TRACK OF TRUST and its fulfillment, the owner's trust becomes stronger and stronger. And my authority could bear the fruit of more freedom for the owner. Think of this early trust and fruit as the "buds" on the vine. More will grow.

In wealth management, trust is so important in helping owners fully release wealth responsibilities to the steward. The more *steward's authority* a client sensed in my services, the easier it was to take *the bridge* across the *chasm of chaos* with all its financial worries and insecurity.

The Steward's Authority: The Voice of "True Riches"

REAPING NEW AUTHORITY, SUCCESS & SWEET PEACE OF MIND

Everyone values good experience in an advisor. But when someone really "delivers" for them personally with the ***steward's authority***, consistently over time, the experience factor rises to a whole new level. A prospective client can "borrow" trust from the steward's "voice" of experience and authority. But when an existing client gets actual experience with the steward, it breeds stronger and stronger trust and confidence.

From the steward's perspective, time and good experience yields even greater authority. It is true that the more they know, the more they know to be concerned about. But through years of faithful service, a true steward is blessed to reap some "true riches" of authority. They know how to deal with most any circumstance that can arise. This is good, faithful experience; not bad, unfaithful experiences repeated over and over like so many ignorant and unwise advisors.

The Bible refers to this, making the point that there is a conditional authority or "riches" that comes to the servant who is honest and trustworthy in the handling of worldly wealth:

> "...whoever is dishonest **with very little** will also be dishonest with much. So if you have not been trustworthy in handling worldly wealth, who will trust you with **true riches**?" (Luke 16:10-11 NIV)

To me the message is clear. The "very little" here is tangible wealth. The "true riches" are intangible wealth. The message implies that a highly responsible steward will be blessed with intangible wealth. I believe the intangible wealth or "true riches" are *truths* and *wisdom*. Some may just call it "good experience." I prefer to call it spiritually inspired insights. Whatever it is, it unlocks authority in the work of *true financial stewards*.

Good experience in handling wealth matters yields new and greater authority with the next set of wealth matters they handle. Stewards of insight and wisdom have a greater chance of financial success in wealth management. Financial success has a particularly sweet perfume to it: *financial peace of mind.*

Just as the aroma of perfume can tend to drift upward, so attending to the "little matters" of the stewardship tends to cause the trust between the client and the servant to spiral up.

So while faithful and wise service of the "little" things breeds more authority and more trust, it also attracts more confidence to delegate by those owners desiring to hire people of true authority and integrity. I call this *the little to much principle.*

It makes sense if you think about it. I was gaining valuable experience and displaying authority in my voice and becoming "attractive" to those who sought genuine leadership in financial and investment matters. When financial success is done the right way, it becomes "a light to the world," so to speak. People sit up and take notice.

THE PRACTICE CAUSE and BONDSERVICE

One day I decided to post in our offices, for all staff and advisors to see, a placard that stated in a few words the purpose of the practice. I called it "The Practice Cause." We posted it in such a way that clients who came into the office could not see it. It read, "To be found good and faithful stewards for our clients; being found trustworthy in both the little things and the much."

The overriding attitude I was trying to instill in any staff member or advisor of the practice was that we should prove ourselves trustworthy in handling the temporal "little things" of others and the "true riches" of new insights and wisdom would be entrusted to us; new authority in our voice. The groundwork I laid in the practice was, "Be found trustworthy in the little things in this stewardship and He will supply the authority that attracts more clients."

The Luke 16 scripture referenced above was a perfect fit because it literally referred to the management of "worldly wealth." I considered the "little things" to be the temporal financial goals and unique interests and values of those owners the practice served. SWM's goal became to manage to achieve the owner's goals, interests, and values.

The emphasis was always, the OWNER'S goals, interests, and values as well as unique concerns.

One thing almost all stewardship stories from the Bible have in common is the steward's focus on the interests of the owner in disregard of his own interests. Hear that again: servants exercising "disregard of their own interests." Wow.

This "bondservice" became the focus of my training of any advisor that would follow me.

With that focus, as well as the practice cause, SWM's *steward's assurance* attempts to deliver highly responsible actions on behalf of clients. Its mantra has become "we can be trusted" and "we will be found faithful."

"CUSTOM BUILDERS": RESPONSE ABILITY

In homebuilding, we call builders who customize home designs for homeowners "custom builders." *True financial stewards* need to be like custom builders.

Responsibilities are like the bricks in the custom home. Authority is like the design itself. The STRONGEST TRUST in wealth management is by custom design. Every owner of wealth has wealth responsibilities; the "bricks." But a person with *steward's authority* knows how to set those "bricks" to fulfill the design. The owner can "hear" this. They hear experience talking. They sense it.

Let's talk about a custom design in wealth management. The more authority, the more knowledge, the more experience an advisor possesses, the more they must "humble themselves" to truly serve. There's an old saying, "Somebody only cares how much we know when they know how much we care."

The owner knows what wealth responsibilities they need built into their custom plans. They just may not know how to see how those "bricks" fit into their financial house; their financial plans. The *steward's authority* through much "design work" in wealth management should "customize" according to the unique financial concerns of each owner.

As the owner and the steward talk, something of the *steward's authority* will stand out to each owner. Something will become key in the TRACK of TRUST being "customized" between them and laid for the steward to run on.

When I think of financial stewardship and the responsibilities to be released by the owner, each responsibility to be "taken over" by the steward faces what I consider the steward's first rule of stewardship. It faces the servant's...

...response ability.

Without response ability on the part of the servant, an owner cannot release this concern into their charge.

If an advisor tries to fit every owner into the advisor's plans, the advisor's molds, perhaps with "model portfolios" or "canned" money management programs, it is as though they have limited or restricted their usefulness to those clients. They have lost the ability to respond differently. It is what I call "response ability."

If this advisor is not open to new and changing tactics and techniques, laws, and/or changes in the financial and investment environments, then they have lost the ability to respond uniquely. Again, lost *response ability*; lost "customization" for the unique values and goals of the client. And owners will find lost authority on the part of the servant who is charged with stewarding plans for the owner.

Owners should beware of advisors who try to fit every owner into one or two molds. Eventually, this mismatch will show up. Most of the time the client is not even aware of it until the advisor's voice loses authority in their ears. This fosters an owner's financial worry instead of peace of mind. Think of it as standing on an emotional *bridge* and looking down into the chasm of financial insecurities.

Remember, as owners, our goal is peace of mind and *full release* to financial freedom. When a steward successfully acknowledges an owner's individual concerns and needs, this *true financial steward* remains able to respond well on behalf of each unique client. They will gain authority in their voice and their service will smell of that perfume of peace.

If we want a Christian advisor as our steward, we want them to have true humility. This is not "door mat" meek. This is possessing authority with flexibility. If our Christian financial steward remains hard or stubborn in their intellectual philosophies, they will lose, or at least resist, the very advantage they have as a spiritually inspired advisor. This is a pride that restricts the ability to be responsible or be "response able." Though a Christian, their lack of response ability to my needs hurts me.

I've come to understand that one of the primary factors in the *steward's authority* is the ability to stay flexible while attempting to be highly responsible. In other words, it is to remain teachable, humble, and a good listener while being able to trust in the knowledge, skills, and experience they possess.

I believe that a sensible, ***response able*** financial steward can give the greatest advantage to those he serves who seek financial peace of mind and *complete* financial freedom.

Trusting the *Steward's Authority* as I Did

If we, as owners, sense the *steward's authority* in their handling of our financial matters, we are more secure. *The steward's authority* paints accurate pictures of what an owner should hope for or expect. This draws out more trust and allows us to exercise more faith in releasing even more responsibilities. If we can develop *high faith* in a partner for our financial future, we will reap peace of mind for a lifetime. Over time, we will be blessed by the *steward's assurance* with *complete* financial freedom.

THE FOUNDATION OF TRUST

What is at the foundation of our trust in an advisor?

This book will show **what** I was seeking and **who** I was seeking to take over "the stewardship" of the practice and of my personal wealth management. It will discuss assurances I needed from them to help me and my clients avoid the dangerous cliffs surrounding financial peace of mind.

I needed to trust the *steward's authority* in helping me customize wise choices for my wealth to help me reach *complete* financial freedom

This book discusses how to avoid taking that LAST FALSE STEP near the three big cliffs surrounding financial peace of mind. It also discusses how to STEP BACK and STEP AROUND toward freedom through the three SAFETY STEPS encouraged in SWM's practice process on behalf of clients.

The reader will learn how certain principles as implemented in the SWM practice process for all its clients, including my wife and me, are worth trusting. They can help people of wealth develop a TRACT OF TRUST for a steward to run on.

Stewards should help owners plan their work and then stewards should be empowered to work the plan just like the owner themselves would.

These principles and this process is what my wife and I trusted.

Finally, the book will share the essence of the "true riches" of assurance I have gleaned over the last 33+ years: the basics of sound financial and smart investment plans, the four keys of ongoing assurances that helps to preserve principal for a lifetime. These principles and processes can be implemented by you.

Or you can learn how to build *high faith* as *the bridge* over the chasm of chaos and fully release all responsibilities for your wealth concerns just as I did.

These are the things my wife and I needed to count on from a steward. We believe our relationship with Ben Dean as a partner in our financial future gives us confidence we will reap peace of mind for a lifetime.

He is a *true financial steward.* He is a *financial freedom provider* for us.

>> CHAPTER 2

THE STEWARD'S ASSURANCE

FOR

COMPLETE

FINANCIAL FREEDOM

Quality in a service or product is not what you put into it.
It is what the client or customer gets out of it.
– PETER DRUCKER

But the greatest among you shall be your servant.
– MATTHEW 23:11

>> THE STEWARD'S ASSURANCE IS A GUARANTEE TO "*BE THERE*" AND USE THE *STEWARD'S AUTHORITY* FOR THE OWNER.

>> WHAT ASSURANCE DO YOU HAVE THAT YOUR INVESTMENT ADVISOR OR BROKER IS STEWARDING YOUR RESOURCES IN SUCH A WAY AS YOU WOULD?

Steve's Story: The Biblical Steward's Assurance

Why do we care what the Bible says and who the Bible says it to?

Well, if the person we hire to manage our wealth is a Christian, he may very well be ruled by more than the money we pay him. He may work for the owner "in sincerity of heart, as to Christ" like I did (Ephesians 6:5-7). He may work as a servant of God first, "in the name of the Lord" like I did (Colossians 3:17). These are the marks of the highly responsible steward we want.

And most importantly for us, the owner, he should offer us the *steward's assurance.*

I OFFERED THE BIBLICAL *STEWARD'S ASSURANCE*

Three verses from the Bible overshadowed my life and the practice cause:

> First, "Whatever you do in word or deed, do all in the name of the Lord." (Colossians 3:17).
>
> Second, "Bondservants, be obedient to those who are your masters according to the flesh, with fear and trembling, in sincerity of heart, AS TO CHRIST...." (Ephesians 6:5-7)
>
> Third, "Whoever can be trusted with very little can also be trusted with much...." (Luke 16:10-11 NIV)

In the preface, my story titled "Positioned to Serve" lays out my professional life just as it happened: My radical conversion to the leadership of Christ, my conviction that as I serve clients, I am doing so "in the name of the Lord."

I had sensed that God wanted me to become a household servant, a steward, for people of wealth so that I could truly help them enjoy *complete* freedom.

As I said before, the practice's story is my story. And my story is the practice's story. SWM promises world-class service and great care for clients' assets. This is the ***steward's assurance***. As you will discover in this book, this involves devotion as well as knowledge, skill, and experience displayed on behalf of their clients.

The ***steward's assurance*** can help the owner step away from the dangerous cliffs and the emotional chasm of chaos around their financial peace of mind and toward *the bridge*. The new destiny is precious and valuable: *complete* financial freedom for the owner.

As the founder of the practice, the premier attitude has always been to be found *true financial stewards* working for clients and being found trustworthy in the very little as well as the much. We would deliver on ***the steward's assurance***. In all my years as a financial advisor, this was my objective and confession.

When the time came to turn my personal wealth over to Ben Dean and the SWM practice process, I knew this was the working attitude of the people serving me. It was a good starting point. It is exactly the attitude we hope for in someone managing our wealth. Right?

Steward's Assurance: "I will BE THERE for you!"

THE PROMISE TO ***DELIVER***

True financial stewards like the practice I developed are worth seeking out. They exist to offer the *steward's assurance* to people of wealth like my wife and me. This is not a guarantee of investment performance, but it is a guarantee of knowledgeable, skilled, experienced, and accountable effort customized for us, the owners.

Simply put, the *steward's assurance* is a guarantee to BE THERE and use the expert generalist authority for the owner. What we have called the *steward's authority*. Yes, it is about intent and about quality, but frankly, as an owner myself, I want delivery.

I want to count on my steward BEING THERE, fully engaged, and fully performing with full authority in the moment of greatest need.

Think of the Olympics. It is one thing for someone to practice, and practice, and practice for an event. We may even say, "Well done" regarding that degree of preparation. But it is another thing to deliver in the moment of greatest testing; the actual Olympic event. Deliver "the Gold"!

In the matter of wealth management, the proof is in the preparation and the planning of expectations. But it is mainly in the events of great testing, such as the first time wealth goes through a "bear" market, or the clients experience a major life change, such as a death, divorce, or full retirement. When wealth goes through the uncertainty of presidential election years and the year after, the equity markets can become exceptionally volatile. The owner should question what the steward delivered in times like those.

The operating philosophy of SWM has always been to **deliver** the *steward's assurance*. They want to **deliver** "the gold" in wealth management. A few years ago the practice had a marketing piece they were developing to explain it.

Marketing: Advertising draft:

Steve Swords is the founder of Swords Wealth Management, LLC. This financial and investment advisory practice was founded on the principle of Christian stewardship. Stewardship is just a good biblical word for fiduciary management.

Some years ago when the Tyler Civic Theatre put down a plaque that described Steve Swords, it did not say he was a CPA or that he had more than 30 years of experience with financial and investment planning. Its readers simply read, "Steve Swords, Financial Steward."

That's what we believe in; being financial stewards for each client's household. That means accepting the extra measure of responsibility to be found faithful and wise in financial matters delegated to us by our clients. To be willing to accept the scrutiny of being transparent managers of the wealth entrusted to us.

It means managing to the client's plans in such a way that the owner would if they had all the desire, time, knowledge, skill, and experience that we possess.

What assurance do you have that your investment advisor or broker is stewarding your resources in such a way as you would?

We craft your plan and we make it easy for you to observe us working your plan. We'll help you fund your goals. You will see times of defense and times of offense with your investments. But mostly, you'll observe what's most important to you: your goals, interests and values being accomplished while you enjoy *complete* financial freedom.

Has your broker or advisor showed you a clear and simple plan of financial management crafted just for you? One that you yourself can see will effectively achieve your values and goals?

Our clients are delegators. Under scrutiny, we will prove we can be trusted and be found faithful to your objectives. Join other clients who have *high faith* in us as a partner in their financial future. Your peace of mind and *complete* financial freedom are not just a hope and a dream. They become our focus. Want help? Let's talk.

Want the *steward's assurance*? Let's get you started today.

[end of ad draft]

Hiring the *Steward's Assurance*

There are practices like SWM and advisors with a heart like mine who offer ***the steward's assurance***.

As I reached my senior years, I began looking for someone just like me to take over this passionate commitment I have for my clients; this "stewardship." This ***steward's assurance***.

I needed a financial advisor who would prove under testing to possess the same attitude and motivation. I needed a true steward for the clients of the practice.

I also needed a true steward for my wife and me. We wanted to release all responsibility for our personal wealth management. Who wants all the responsibilities of dealing with personal wealth if they know they can delegate those concerns away? And I knew *true financial stewards* exist and hiring one is the only way to *complete* freedom. My wife and I wanted ***the steward's assurance*** for our own peace of mind.

I Hired a *True Financial Steward* & You Can To

As mentioned in Chapter 1, highly responsible stewards do exist. And unlike do-it-yourselfers who believe no one would be as responsible for their financial well-being as they would, I knew better.

I knew we could hire a servant who will be as responsible for our wealth as we would. In this book I will show you how I did it.

As I was entering my retirement years, I made a decision to entrust my wealth management to Ben Dean. I would not have done this had I not tested and proven Ben. As I said above, my wife and I wanted to release all responsibility for our personal wealth management. We were willing to delegate to a *true financial steward.* We were consenting to "a little," in hope to release much, much more. We wanted the best: *complete* financial freedom. We were looking for a highly responsible advisor.

First and foremost, we wanted a person who was a professional.

But in addition to that, we needed a person who would be servant-hearted in their approach. Would he be flexible and able to respond to our unique values and needs? Would he customize certain matters just for us? Would he treat our engagement with the firm like a personal stewardship between us and him?

Highly responsible stewards are people that we can count on to manage our affairs with authority. They take such delegated responsibilities seriously. A person of authority will demand thorough, solid financial plans focused on our core values and key financial goals. They will demand smart investments for growth of our accumulated wealth. They will demand monitoring of market risk and proactively defending accumulated wealth.

My question was whether Ben would be all these things. In short, would Ben offer us the ***steward's assurance***?

>> CHAPTER 3

FINDING MY *COMPLETE* FINANCIAL FREEDOM

I FOUND A *TRUE FINANCIAL STEWARD*

...the one who is the greatest among you must become like the youngest, and the leader like the servant.

– LUKE 22:26

>> IN EARLY 2014, I BEGAN TO LOOK FOR A FINANCIAL ADVISOR TO WORK WITH ME....

>> ONE WHO WOULD HAVE A CERTAIN HEART COMMITMENT.

>> ONE WHO COULD TAKE OVER THE SERVICE OF THE FIRM'S CLIENTS AS WELL AS THAT OF MY WIFE AND ME.

>> HE BECAME MY *TRUE FINANCIAL STEWARD* AND MY FAMILY'S PARTNER IN PURSUIT OF OUR *COMPLETE* FINANCIAL FREEDOM.

Steve's Story: I Found a Protégé Who Is a *True Financial Steward*.

To a certain extent, sometimes "the greatest among" us "must become like the youngest" (Luke 22:26). Or as I like to say, "The greatest is often the student of the good." So it was when my search for a true financial steward led me to Ben Dean. I knew exactly what I was looking for on behalf of both my clients and my wife and me.

In early 2014, I began to look for a financial advisor to work with me: One who would have a certain heart commitment to the work; someone who would be of like mind with me.

I had reached my senior years and I sensed a change coming in my working life. I needed a person worthy of strong trust to take over "the stewardship" I had with my clients. I needed a steward for them. And I needed one for my wife and me.

I knew that using a *true financial steward* is the only way to *complete* financial freedom. And, as I said before, my wife and I wanted to fully release the financial responsibilities of our personal wealth.

PRAYER AND PROVISION OF A STEWARD

One morning I found myself praying, "Lord, I need you to send me someone who can help share the burden of this stewardship. Someone you trust to care for them as I move on to the next season of your purposes for me."

Within 24 hours, Ben Dean had called me to catch up on what had been going on in our lives. Soon the conversation turned to the thought he had of possibly joining me in my firm in east Texas. The short version of that exchange is that he joined me as a laborer and advisor within the practice.

I didn't tell him about my prayer for another six months. During that time he followed my every move, participated in every client meeting, and proved to be teachable in the unique facets of true financial stewardship just as I had walked before the Lord for more than 30 years. In a sense, though he had much knowledge and skill, he became my protégé working together with me. He didn't know it, but I was testing him.

THE PROCESS OF RELEASE

When I began my discovery process to determine if Ben was truly a good fit for my clients and for my personal wealth management, several important questions were going through my mind:

- Would he have a genuine heart to serve? Did he work with a conscience? In other words, would he "work as unto the Lord"?

- Would he be able to assure me and my clients we could fully release wealth responsibilities to him?
  - Had he reaped enough "true riches" in wisdom and insight from his prior advisory experience that I could sense *the steward's authority* in his voice?
  - Would he show himself highly responsible to carry the cares of our wealth responsibilities?

- Would he have the emotional, intellectual, social, and professional commitment to "be there" for our wealth management so I wouldn't need to be?

  - Would his *stewardship assurance* include that he would work my or my clients' financial plans the way that we would if we were there?

- Would he help me and my clients to develop STRONG TRUST by clearly establishing **what** to expect and **how** he would respond?
  - Would he help us define expectations and then help us spot true experiences that would lead us to stronger and stronger trust and *high faith*?

- Would I and my clients think him worthy of delegation of all our assets as he showed himself different from worldly wealth managers only selfishly interested in building their "Assets Under Management"?
  - Would he prove to be a true "bondservant" focusing on my interests in disregard of his own?

- Would he show the ability to customize my financial plans, being flexible enough to respond differently for my wife and me than for other clients?
  - Would he craft a clear and simple plan of financial management just for my household?
  - And could he show the capability to do unique plans for each client?

Not only were these questions critical for the hope and trust I needed in someone who would replace me, but some tests of these issues were needed. This process would become the foundation of this book. In essence, how would he help me and my clients step toward *the bridge* to *complete* financial freedom, step away from the emotional cliffs of the chasm surrounding peace of mind, and help us fully release worries about financial resources?

When Ben Dean came to work with me, although he had plenty of financial experience, I needed to confirm that we shared an approach to client services that involved biblical stewardship. His responses in this book will illustrate his convictions.

In this book, I will describe much of the process that I have taken Ben through in discerning his stewardship and in testing his trustworthiness. Could he be the chief steward for each client he would serve in the practice that I founded? Could he serve my wife and me during our retirement years?

WHO AND WHAT "COMPLETES ME"

This book describes the process of defining, finding, and testing Ben as a potential *true financial steward*; one who could give those he serves *complete* financial freedom. It describes not only the **who** I wanted, but the **what** I needed:

First, was he a person of knowledge, skill, and experience?

Second, was he a highly responsible person?

Third, would he develop well-defined financial plans with teeth? One which set personal demands on the owners as well as giving reasonable expectations of what to expect from his management and defense of our plans?

Fourth, would he know how to help us develop a TRACK of TRUST; reasonable expectations in both the uncontrollable as well as controllable aspects of financial life? We wanted him to name specific things we could observe him handling.

Fifth, would he have the skill to help preserve the wealth entrusted to him, the owner's personal lifestyles or estates in our retirement years?

In short, would he give us certain *steward assurances* that we could achieve financial peace of mind while releasing the cares of our wealth management to him?

By late 2014, he had proved to be the *true financial steward* I knew we needed. He became my partner and a person whom I trust to share the burden of the stewardship of the clients of Swords Wealth Management, LLC. He became my *true financial steward* and my family's partner in pursuit of our *complete* financial release.

Ben's Story:

I met Steve while employed at my previous firm. Our relationship goes back to May of 2008. I remember my first face-to-face meeting with Steve. It was during a random branch office review that my firm sent me to conduct in his office. I sent the audit agenda and my requirements to his office ahead of time.

When I arrived, I discovered that Steve and his staff had meticulously prepared everything I requested. They handed me the completed package with a large file of back up documentation. This was very unusual for the offices I visited. His office had complied with everything I needed. I thought to myself, "Wow, this practice is different." They seemed really helpful to me. I would learn this was the servant-hearted approach Steve sought to inspire in every staff member, advisor, and endeavor of the practice.

His strong Christian values and dedication to thorough work on behalf of clients are the reasons I wanted to join him. When I began working with them, I learned much more about why this practice seemed different. They wanted to be *true financial stewards.*

I was willing to listen and learn as he spoke as one with authority and not as any other advisor I had ever known. Becoming his partner has not stopped his coaching of me as we make our mutual quest to be found faithful and wise servants on behalf of our clients.

Henry David Thoreau in his book *Walden* says, "A man is rich in proportion to the number of things which he can afford to let alone." This is a fitting quote for delegators in relation to their financial stewards. And it fits with what Steve is trying to do for his wife and himself as well as for his clients. My hope is that I am making him "rich" in freedom as he releases more and more wealth responsibilities to me. This is my hope for all my clients.

I've always thought of stewardship as the act of trying to be found "good and faithful." We should to be found trustworthy in both the little things and the much.

This principle fits right in with who I am. As I went through our financial roadmap conversation with Steve and his wife, I thought about and documented what it is that is really important to them. In other words, what it is that gives them joy and what was their *chasm of concerns*?

Only after knowing and understanding these important things was I able to formulate an appropriate and attainable plan for him and his wife based on clear, reasonable expectations. These are key to their financial plan of action, a kind of roadmap for their finances; a bridge to their financial peace of mind.

In this book we offer a roadmap to *complete* financial freedom. If you can develop STRONG TRUST and high faith in a highly responsible person as Steve and his wife have done in me, you too can successfully cross the *chasm of financial concerns* and experience *complete* freedom.

>> CHAPTER 4

3 BIG CLIFFS BLOCKING FINANCIAL PEACE OF MIND

Let us not be defeated by the tyranny of the world financial markets that threaten peace and democracy everywhere.
– STÉPHANE HESSEL, *French Diplomat and Concentration Camp Survivor*

A man always has two reasons for what he does--a good one, and the real one.
– J.P. MORGAN

And who of you by being worried can add a single hour to his life? ...do not worry about tomorrow; for tomorrow will care for itself. Each day has enough trouble of its own.
– MATTHEW 6:27, 34

>> WHETHER SPENDING TOO MUCH OR WORRYING TOO MUCH, BOTH ARE SIMPLY TOO MUCH.

>> TO DEVELOP STRONG TRUST WE NEED EXPECTATIONS THAT ARE TESTED OVER TIME AND ARE ACCURATE IN THE EXPERIENCE OF SOMEONE WHO HAS THE TRUE SKILL TO MANAGE RESPONSIBILITIES WITH AUTHORITY.

>> AT THE CORE OF CLIFF #3, "POOR DELEGATION OF WEALTH CONCERNS" IS A LACK OF POSITIVE, TRUSTWORTHY EXPERIENCES. "BLIND FAITH" IS THE FATHER OF BAD EXPERIENCES AND RESULTS IN CONTINUING FINANCIAL WORRIES. THIS CHASM IS DEEP.

Steve's Story: The *Chasm of Chaos*

What do you do in a world of chaos? In a world where financial markets seem manipulated and financial advisors seem selfish? How do we find peace of mind in our financial plans? How do we retire with a reasonable assurance of financial peace of mind for life?

In my 30 years in the ministry of serving investment clients, I've never seen the investment world in as much chaos as it has been from 2008 to 2016. Everybody has an opinion. There is no real certainty of many matters because the future is not so nearly like the past as it used to be.

We used to be concerned mainly with the U.S. economy. After all it was one of the world's largest economies. But now, we have to be concerned with all economies in the world.

The world has become a smaller, more integrated place. With the advent of high speed computers and smart phones putting the "World Wide Web" at our fingertips many are confused by the information overload.

We must consider currency changes, the interest-rate environment, banking concerns, countries in debt default, hyperinflation in some countries and no inflation in others. We also recognize market manipulation by those, too often, self-serving political or central banking authorities, afraid of losing their jobs.

Spending and savings plans in flux are the norm as more and more job insecurity becomes a reality. Should we trust our employers who drop us on a moment's notice? Should we trust our industry leaders, politicians, or investment bankers? These regulate costly services and control the flow of funds to our households, whether it be business economies, employee wages, bank credit, or regulated expenses like utilities or medical costs.

Where did we lose control of our own financial destiny? When did the hope of the "American Dream" become the expectation of an American nightmare? Financial concerns and outright anxiety seem to abound. Financial peace of mind is blocked by an emotional *chasm of chaos*: a chasm of concerns and financial worries as dangerous cliffs that can lead to despair.

But this chasm can be crossed. The cliffs can be turned away from. Financial peace of mind is reachable.

To help manage around this chaos, we need men or women of true financial *steward's authority*. I'm reminded of the Bible verse that describes Jesus as a person of authority: "When Jesus had finished these words, the crowds were amazed at His teaching; for He was teaching them as one having authority, and not as their scribes." (Matthew 7:28-29)

If we find a *true financial steward*, we find one "having authority."

Ben's Response:

As the average citizen experiences more mandated taxes, and as insurance and other related laws become more complex, it is easy for uncertainty to become the only certainty.

Did anybody, including politicians, really know what we were in for when what's known as the "Obamacare" act was first passed?

Financial worry, or any worry for that matter, is more often than not a lack of sound thinking and plans in a world of financial chaos. Without a broad enough thinking-through process to resolve our own insecurities, confidence lags. Often *Do-it-yourselfers* miss some essential GOOD planning steps and concepts. In addition, their undisciplined plans may leave them open to the big cliffs discussed below.

Steve: The 3 Big Cliffs of the *Chasm of Chaos*

Having counseled clients through retirement successfully countless times, we know that "false steps" in financial and investment planning are numerous and broad. However, in our experience, three dangerous cliffs can leave us stumbling into a *chasm of chaos* where financial peace of mind seems hopeless.

And, of course, as around any cliff, a single short step in the wrong direction can be devastating.

Cliff #1: Spending Based on Poor Life$tyle Estimates

It is amazing how we act before we ever try to account for our real annual spending. Not our income. Our average household expenses on an annual basis.

In planning long-term lifestyle, we are not so much suggesting "budgeting" as we are estimating general future annual spending given inflation, taxes, life expectancy, rate of return on investment, etc.

Many times, during the working years, wage earners set "budgets" around what they earn. They will subconsciously think that the same should be true in the future. "Just match our spending to our income and everything will be okay. Right?"

Unfortunately, because of the many complexities of long-term forecasting, trying to keep lifestyle estimates that simple can be hazardous. Many will even treat it as a mental exercise.

Speaking of hazardous mental exercises, there's a fable of a guy who went to Las Vegas with a plan not to lose a dime. He would gamble, but only in his mind. Unfortunately, he lost his mind.

If all we do is mental planning, we may lose our mind. Mental planning, even "rough" pen scratching on a pad, is insufficient. And because the exercise is truly complex, many will abandon it altogether.

Or try to throw more income at it. After all, "more income makes everything perfect. Right?" If my life is lived around the pursuit of more income, more often than not, it is a very sad life. It may work well during the "good" years, but sooner or later things change.

As with all cliffs, as we approach this one, a "false step" could cast us into an emotional chasm. The deep *chasm of chaos* with its anxieties can destroy our peace of mind.

Let's discuss the two most common stumbling blocks:

- Spending too much thinking, "I have plenty," or
- Worrying too much thinking, "I don't have enough."

SPENDING TOO MUCH THINKING "I HAVE PLENTY"

We may think and act like we have all the money we will ever need; spending too much. The truth is that we don't know what the future holds. It seems it takes some aging for most people to learn this lesson.

Left unrestrained "the seed corn" principle comes into play. If we eat up all the corn, we have no seed for next year's planting. It is okay to eat some of the corn seed, what some call our "principal," but never TOO MUCH of it.

The false step is not knowing when to stop, STEP BACK, and STEP AROUND this cliff.

We all know people who have outspent their resources and gotten deep in debt. That is all true debt comes down to; long-term spending in excess of long-term resources. It is a cliff. And it destroys financial peace of mind.

WORRY TOO MUCH THINKING,"I DON'T HAVE ENOUGH"

We may think and act like we will never have enough; *worrying too* much. For lack of good lifestyle forecasts, or failure to really LOOK at good estimates, this person is often found saying, "We can't afford it." If this is me, it is possible I have other reasons I am saying this, but often I'm just convinced, "We can't plan." This too is a "cliff."

The false step is continuing to step off this "cliff" when we should stop, STEP BACK, and STEP AROUND. A wise quote from the Bible admonishes us:

> *"Who of you by being worried can add a single hour to his life?* (Matthew 6:27*)*
>
> *"...do not worry about tomorrow; for tomorrow will care for itself."* (Matthew 6:34a)

Whether spending too much or worrying too much, both are simply TOO MUCH. These are syndromes of spending based upon poor lifestyle estimates. Or on not really "paying attention to" the estimates we have.

Obviously, sometimes we need a governor on our spending, but sometimes we just need to stop worrying. A good analysis of *lifestyle spending* on an annual basis with the proper assumptions can help us avoid worry and let us employ discipline in our spending habits.

Cliff #2: Making Quick and Poor Decisions

It is one of the most enticing and seductive things in life to face a buying opportunity without a sound plan. It might be a lip-smacking stock tip, an exquisite piece of jewelry, a new car sale, a super-discounted RV, or a rare buy on raw land. We all have financial temptations, but the choices we make too quickly can destroy financial peace of mind.

We hear of "winging it." This is a false step around this dangerous "cliff." We must stop, STEP BACK, and STEP AROUND or we will end up with poor decisions; decisions that do not reflect our true values. We can be found tumbling into the chasm of much deeper financial concerns.

Sometimes this is an individual's "cliff" and not the couple's. Mutually agreed upon accountability to a long-term plan is most important if one tends to "wing it" all too often. And let's admit it. We know who we are. While we are rational, set a plan and agree to stick with it.

Financial problems typically come when we don't have that intermediate or long-term financial "plumb line." A "plumb line" is the thing a carpenter or brick mason uses. They may chalk up a string and "pop" a line on the floor or a wall. This plumb line enables them to keep things on track.

Sometimes financial worry suddenly "is there." It is like running through forest bushes and breaking out into the open just as our feet come sliding to the edge of a chasm. The cliff biting at our toes.

Chaotic daily living can do that to us. We simply violate our financial plans with quick decisions that do not consider the longer-term impact. Then later, an internal gnawing gives way to the stark reality: "too much month at the end of the money."

Seldom do these quick decisions turn out profitable. Justifiable? Yes. Absolutely. We are probably building our irrational case to present to our spouse or our conscience even before the first lusty thought has time to settle. Profitable? Normally, no. Especially against the backdrop of financial peace of mind.

Failing to plan ahead can lead to false steps ending up in quick and wrong decisions with long-term impact. For example, in 2000,

2001, and 2002 investment markets became very unfriendly. The quick decision most amateurs made was "leave everything alone." During that time frame, the world lost trillions of dollars of wealth. Many individual households lost 30% to 50% of their personal investment value over those three years. And many have still not recovered nearly fifteen years later.

Why? Without an exit plan for invested assets, a series of uneducated, unplanned quick decisions said, "Leave everything alone."

Cliff #3: Poor Delegation of Wealth Concerns

Imagine a widow who lives in a big house. Plush. Very comfortable though showing its age a bit. Like so many retired investors, she senses that the investment world is not the same as it had been in the past 25 years while her husband was alive. A deep concern, perhaps even fear, holds her in financial worry about her future. There seems to be no way around this *chasm of* what could seem to her a *chaos* of constant changes. "Who has answers? Who can really help me?" she worries.

Too often our relative or best buddy or the guy in the seat next to us is the wrong person to listen to for smart choices about our financial future. It is as if some think wisdom is okay with discounting of knowledge, skill, and experience in the pursuit of social relationships and *best buddy advice.* Excuse me, but this is not wisdom speaking.

Many people lack the knowledge, skill, or experience, or even the time, needed to do longer-term financial and investment planning and management that can give them lasting peace of mind. They know deep inside that they lack any real authority and skill in this area.

Many times it is just our pride that leads us down this wrong path. I have never flown a plane but once asked a pilot of a major airline if he would mind if I flew his big DC-10 passenger jet –

with him in it! Of course, he chuckled at that. I have no authority as a pilot.

In a similar way, a surgeon wouldn't try to operate on himself and a smart defendant wouldn't try to represent himself in court.

The false step here is failure to delegate when we should. We must stop, STEP BACK, and STEP AROUND this "cliff."

Weak trust of otherwise good financial advisors and the related financial worry is often merely the result of a lack of *clear expectations*. Once those expectations are defined, we often still may not release responsibility to those men or women of true financial authority. We call this *the delegate and release PROBLEM*.

Of course, it is normal that ultimate responsibility still resides with the owner, but the smart money knows the importance of delegating and fully releasing responsibilities to the delegate. A *true financial steward* is a person of skill and authority who can relieve the owner of the broad concerns of responsibilities with wealth.

Ultimately, once trust grows stronger and stronger in that person, the owner will feel less financial worry. We are stepping away from the emotional cliff, the chasm of wealth concerns, as financial freedom becomes a daily reality.

Delegated Representatives: Choose Wisely with this Power

Where can we get help in time of need? Who can be trusted to whom key financial decisions might be delegated?

Household owners seeking financial assistance can find advisors of various types. These are differentiated mostly by their compensation. Various compensation methods include:

- **Commissioned** (i.e., a securities broker makes 5% on a mutual fund sale or an agent for an insurance company makes 5% to 80% of first-year premiums)
- **commissions and fees**, or
- **fee only** (i.e. an advisor charges a percentage against assets, an asset-based fee, or a flat fee for a plan).

For the most part, *the steward's assurance*, which regulators refer to as "the fiduciary role" using terms like "supervision" and investment "oversight," is found only with *registered investment advisors.* These normally are "fee only" advisors.

The key to *wise choices* is to understand that the "fee only" advisor is trying to establish a longer-term relationship with his or her client. They are not nearly so interested in the upfront compensation. Unfortunately, their attention to the client's needs and concerns may end once the assets are "in the account."

The important consideration here is not so much their method of compensation as it is whether they truly have the type of character to help us bridge the chaos without worry.

Ben's Response:

Traditionally, advisors have delivered financial services with an *old world* view focused on transactions, commissions and obtaining as many clients as possible.

Today, *new world* advisors can be found focusing on relationships and on-going services. However, many are focused only on building "assets under management" or AUM. These advisors have little respect for the idea of household focused stewardship.

Unfortunately, this is part of the nature of the business. Having higher AUM is highly valued by the biggest and best custodians and brokerage houses. Of course, big custodians are often best for advisors.

Therefore, to avoid being just a number or AUM on some advisor's roll call, some additional screening is necessary by the person searching for a steward. Especially when trying to delegate responsibilities that are tied to our financial peace of mind.

Steve: On The Delegate and Release PROBLEM: "blind faith"

As owners, our lack of knowledge with long-term financial and investment planning may dictate we "delegate" those responsibilities. But a person may still hold financial worry tightly if they fail to "release" those responsibilities. True financial freedom is almost impossible without full release as well as delegation.

In a world of self-centered financial advisors, it is easy for owners to have no peace of mind because of what we call *the delegate and release PROBLEM* of "blind faith." Ultimately, it is no delegation at all and results in financial worry rather than peace of mind.

Many advisers would like us to simply have "blind faith" in their services.

No questions. No expectations. No accountability.

At the core of Cliff #3, "Poor Delegation of Wealth Concerns," is a lack of positive, trustworthy experiences. "Blind faith" is the father of bad experiences and results in continuing financial worries. This chasm is deep.

Of course, the default of taking no action is making no delegation decision despite knowing we should. So no delegation also continues financial anxiety and the chasm seems insurmountable without a bridge.

STRONG TRUST, NO ACTION INSECURITY

At the risk of sounding "preachy," financial anxiety will not go away without trust. And while trust is an emotion, it only gives relief from worry if acted upon. So we need both trust and discipline. This is really what "faith" is. In order to make good choices, we need both trust and faith, or "trust in action."

It is possible to believe strongly, even trust strongly, and yet never take action; exercise no discipline. Strong trust with no action is no faith and does no good.

WEAK TRUST, "BLIND FAITH," FINANCIAL WORRY

But merely meeting with a financial advisor and hiring them will not bridge the chasm of our concerns. In other words, not all actions are based on STRONG TRUST.

It is possible to act without any real confidence; with insufficient belief or experience. This is acting in "blind faith." Many will throw up a prayer and act without true hope.

This normally sets the stage for insecurity. WEAK TRUST, "blind faith" is like walking near the cliff. And anxiousness and worry is a deep chasm.

In the financial world, delegating with WEAK TRUST and a poor release of responsibility allows financial anxiety to continue. We may mask it or bury it deep in the recesses of our thoughts, but it is there. It is like standing longer and longer on the edge of that cliff. Once again, STEP BACK, and STEP AROUND the cliff and look for *the bridge.*

LACKING CLEARLY DEFINED & REASONABLE EXPECTATIONS

Why do WEAK TRUST and "blind faith" play a part in many financial decisions? Normally, it stems from lack of experience and knowledge. But it can be the result of failing to have *clearly defined* and *repeatable, reasonable* expectations; sometimes by choice; sometimes by ignorance.

For many, something inside us just begs to know what we can expect. It is as though expectations are the road signs on a highway. As we pass certain mile markers or landmarks, these road signs encourage our trust that we are on the right path. Our trust rises. It gets stronger.

And something inside us needs to sense decisions are made with authority, not mere hope.

But financial advisors today have developed the skill to get us to decide to do something without trustworthiness even being a factor. Their sales techniques may have us wondering when we leave their office why we agreed to work with them. They have duped us into “blind faith.”

"Blind faith" is doing something “just because.” It is a decision “just because.” And it is not smart because it is based on WEAK TRUST. Once again...

...No questions. No expectations. No accountability.

This should not be so. Remember, this is where deep financial anxiety comes from. Nobody likes sleeping in a car while another drives, only to wake up and see no road signs we expected to see. “Are we lost?” is an expression of insecurity.

What we want as owners is STRONG TRUST based on *clear, reasonable expectations*. Even if we are inclined to stay in the dark, we should embrace that expectations are good light. They yield *financial peace of mind.*

Ben’s Response:

The Y2K phenomenon of the late 1990s is a great example of “blind faith” in action. My story shows the stark contrast of “blind faith” based on WEAK TRUST and how we developed STRONG TRUST in *clear, reasonable expectations.*

At a previous firm, I was tasked with preparing our firm's computers for the new millennium. As I called around to other professional firms, I quickly learned that many businesses were not doing any planning at all. Other firms were addressing the problem with only a halfhearted approach. Both seemed to me to be entirely inadequate. They were exercising "blind faith" that their computer systems would be fine. To me, it was a very weak trust proposition and made me "insecure" about our computers being okay.

Some people settle with this type of mere hope and prayer. I wanted a greater assurance.

In the next chapter, under the topic "the Delegate and Release FREEDOM," I will share with you how we went from mere hope to STRONG TRUST by being much more diligent. The pattern of developing STRONG TRUST, SMART CHOICES, and faith in a process is a pattern clients of *true financial stewards* get to experience. We will find that it involves building a set of test experiences into a stronger and stronger trust as those experiences turn into *clear, reasonable expectations* upon which we can put trust in action.

>> CHAPTER 5

3 SAFETY STEPS TO *FINANCIAL PEACE OF MIND*

By teaching twenty-something-year-olds responsible debt management practices, we can help them create a balanced lifestyle and find peace of mind through increased financial awareness, smart saving and long-term investing.

– ALEXA VON TOBEL, Financially Fearless

Founder of LearnVest.com

Financial peace isn't the acquisition of stuff. It is learning to live on less than you make, so you can give money back and have money to invest. You can't win until you do this.

– DAVE RAMSEY, National best-selling author and radio host, *America's trusted voice on money*

The mind of man plans his way, But the LORD directs his steps.

– PROVERBS 16:9

>> AS THE WISDOM SCRIPTURE IMPLIES, PLANS CAN BE ADJUSTED IN "MID-STREAM," BUT YOU HAVE TO START WITH A PLAN.

>> FINANCIAL WORRY CAN FADE AWAY. THAT IS, IF WE CAN YIELD TO A NEW STRONG TRUST.

>> THE HIGHEST LEVEL OF FINANCIAL FREEDOM COMES IN STEPPING TOWARD AND CROSSING *THE BRIDGE* TO FINANCIAL PEACE OF MIND AND FULL RELEASE OF WEALTH RESPONSIBILITIES.

Steve's Story: Plan with God's Help!

There is something very comforting about solid, sound financial plans. There is also something soothing about having God on our side. Christians believe He guides us. A wisdom scripture from His bible in Proverbs says, "The mind of man plans his way, but the LORD directs his steps." (Proverbs 16:9)

Notice that wisdom expects man's part is to PLAN. For Christians, we always remain alert to the Lord's redirecting. Nevertheless, we should plan.

Financial Peace of Mind Clarified

A long time ago, it was made clear to me that a lot of *financial peace of mind* comes in having sound, clear plans. It is essential in rising above the financial chaos that plans anticipate real life circumstances: things like life expectancy, taxes, inflation, changing return of investments, and even unexpected emergency spending.

Keep in mind, as the wisdom scripture implies, plans can be adjusted in "midstream," but you have to start with a plan.

A written plan that can be recalled in the midst of our yet uncertain, but happening, day by day future is the best. The plan recall process is key. Regularly scheduled progress reviews are essential. And key assumptions are to be tested.

We start with what it is we want to happen if "such-and-such" circumstance occurs. Then, when it does, we respond with, "This-and-that is what we will do because such-and-such has happened." A *true financial steward* can be of great help with this.

Once we are confident that our financial "such-and-suches" are planned for, financial worry can fade away. We are beginning to step away from the *chasm of concerns*. That is, if we can develop and yield to a new STRONG TRUST. We are trusting that future "such-and-suches" are predictable. If that is not true for us, we need help. We may have to put our confidence in a professional. Eventually, the highest level of financial freedom comes in stepping toward and crossing *the bridge* to financial peace of mind and full release of wealth responsibilities.

If our *chasm of concerns* is fostered by poor planning, quick decisions or insufficient knowledge, skill or experience and the failure to delegate, then to hire and test a financial steward is a major step toward *the bridge*.

Ben's Response:

Most people do little if any thorough, sound planning. And many who plan make decisions based on poor planning or poor *plan recall*. These simple-to-correct mistakes made over and over again cost them valuable resources needed for financial peace of mind.

That is where professionals such as Swords Wealth Management, LLC (www.swordswealthmanagement.com) should come in. We are worthy of STRONG TRUST and offer the promise of financial peace of mind to those that release the concerns of being responsible with wealth to us.

Steve: On Offering *Peace of Mind*

Most individual households lack the knowledge, skills, or experience to be able to handle their own financial management in a world of chaos and turmoil; a world that requires timely responses to our event risks and changing market trends. The *chasm of chaos* is deep and wide with many, many facets of financial concern.

Why deal with the huge learning curve and possible costly "experience" lessons?

The so-called "smart money" people hire smart, highly responsible people. A highly responsible steward, who will possess broad knowledge, honed skills, and good experience, can offer true peace of mind to those seeking help. These responsible persons are exactly who we want: people of *steward's authority* who give us a sense of assurance.

Ben's Response:

In 1989, I was working for a financial services company that catered to CPAs. I realized that joining the trust inherent with CPAs with a highly responsible advisor in broad financial and investment matters gave clients the STRONG TRUST they needed for financial peace of mind. This is when I decided to pursue the Certified Financial Planner or CFP® designation. I wanted to be that smart, highly responsible practitioner.

Being certified to practice financial planning since 1993 has afforded me experience through several different economic and business cycles. The more experience I gained, the more authority I heard coming from my own voice. I sincerely believe financial planning is more crucial than ever. It is a noble business to serve with authority and with professionalism in financial and investment planning.

The financial guidance and a cooperative effort between a *true financial steward* and his client make a positive difference in the owner's lives. We love it when a certain settling or assurance comes to those we serve in the midst of their personal *chasm of concerns*. They see a chasm. We see *the bridge*.

Steve: On Stepping Back from the Cliffs

The relationship between a steward and the owner is built on a set of *clear, reasonable expectations*. Let's call this the TRACK of TRUST. Simply put, both the steward and the owner must stay on the steps of this TRACK of TRUST in order to avoid the cliffs between where we are and where we are going.

Financial peace of mind is not out of reach. In Chapter 4 we discussed three dangerous cliffs that can leave us stumbling into a *chasm of concerns* where financial peace of mind seems hopeless. And, of course, as around any cliff, just a single short step in the wrong direction can be devastating.

Similarly, a single short step in the right direction can save us. A choice to stop, STEP BACK, and STEP AROUND the "cliff" can lead us to safety and, ultimately, put us back on a good path. Think of these as ***safety steps***. Each short safety step in the right direction could be the most important "next" single step in our financial life.

Safety Step #1: STEP BACK and STEP AROUND Spending based on Poor Life$tyle Forecasts

Whether we spend TOO MUCH or worry TOO MUCH, generally, both are symptoms of spending based on a poor understanding of our future estimated annual needs. To help us step away from this "cliff," it is important to have a well-defined financial plan and a model to help manage that plan.

To STEP BACK and STEP AROUND this cliff it is important to understand how financial goals that require money are being planned for in our future time line.

True financial stewards will plan financial resources to be available to us to consume at different times over our life. The more we understand when and where, the more personal restraint we will put upon ourselves not to violate our plans.

THE ASSUMPTIONS & THE OWNER'S RESPONSIBILITY

A well-defined plan involves a number of long-term assumptions. It is the individual household owner's responsibility to understand how their financial goals and their long-term assumptions interact. In particular, if assumptions become inaccurate over time, lifestyle adjustments may be needed.

A good financial model will have the ability to easily adjust our plan and to see how changing assumptions would impact our expected outcome. This is crucial to being able to judge expectations by actual experiences and, ultimately, build stronger and stronger trust in our assumptions about the future. The *true financial steward* will have tools to help us do exactly that.

Clear, reasonable expectations lead us to STRONG TRUST and SMART CHOICES. This is how we walk across *the bridge* and over the *chasm of our concerns*.

Ben's Response:

When meeting with our existing clients, we always review their financial plan. We cover their goals that require money outside of their routine lifestyle spending.

Routine lifestyle spending is also discussed to verify that the client is adhering to their goal of spending within their means. The review of the impact of their lifestyle on long-term plans is a not so subliminal reminder of their part in the task of not outspending their resources. Control your life$tyle.

Stepping toward *the bridge* to *complete* financial freedom starts with this discipline.

Steve: On...

Safety Step #2: STEP BACK and STEP AROUND Quick Decisions

Often some of the most costly financial decisions are ones that are made quickly or based on poor information in violation of our own intermediate to longer-term plans. To avoid this cliff, begin making SMART CHOICES instead of quick decisions.

Most of the time, SMART CHOICES are just a matter of training on how to use a sound financial and investment plan. We must all understand the three simple steps in working with financial plans as addressed in more detail in Chapter 8. But a few starting keys can put Safety Step #2 in effect immediately.

PLAN LONG-TERM

To overcome the financial chaos that often results from quick or poor decisions, we should NOT ONLY have a well-defined plan, but that plan should be long-term.

We consider a long-term plan to be two to 25 years in duration.

Obviously, many of the assumptions over that long a time horizon will change. Smart financial advisors and all *true financial stewards* will attempt to break that time horizon into smaller components; say five-year increments.

This makes our long-term plans somewhat intermediate-term in nature. They can be used to plan routine spending needs and liquidity for other financial needs over the next two to five years.

What will our savings and/or spending look like over the next two to five years?

In our *pre-retirement* years, the question may be, how much can we save each year?

In the *post-retirement* years, other questions arise. Will we need investment money for extraordinary things such as home improvements, major travel, car replacements, or funding grandchildren's college expenses? We call these *liquidity needs*.

PLAN to DEFEND the PLAN

Further, it is important to have someone designated to defend the plan. This means, if we want freedom or otherwise don't trust ourselves to manage our lifestyle around our goals and long-term financial assumptions, then we get help. We may want to make sure our financial delegate is not afraid to advise us to stick with our plan.

If we call up to get money in advance of a scheduled liquidity need, a *true financial steward* will advise us we are violating our plan. As we like to say, "It takes guts to confront the owner against his own quick decisions."

Owners should consider clearly saying to our delegate, "I want you to tell me if my lifestyle spending and other financial goals are too big for my resources." Or try this: "How will my request for unplanned cash impact me in the long term?"

Of course, as the owner, we may truly feel we need to change our long-term assumptions. Perhaps our lifestyle spending has increased due to inflation, or we have reassessed our original estimate of monthly needs.

What if we have no other choice – we really need a cash withdrawal now. Though it was unexpected, we know it is the only option. We recognize it will impact our long-term plans. That's OK. Plans should always be "adjustable" around such circumstances.

On the other hand, if we want our long term plan to stay "as is" and/or if the cash withdrawal is optional, we should want our financial steward to defend the plan against changing choices. He or she is helping us assure the plan is worked and working toward our financial peace of mind.

We must be sure to empower stewards to *talk truth* to us.

The idea is clear: ***Have a plan. Work the plan***.

Ben's Response:

One of our more difficult conversations with clients revolves around "out of plan" expenditures. We have a financial model of planned expenditures for each client. While we are able to be flexible to and assess the impact of "out of plan" expenditures, we do strive to help clients stay on a reasonable path of their original plan.

Steve: On...

Safety Step #3: STEP BACK and STEP AROUND Delegation in "blind faith"

Failure to delegate wealth management, when we lack the knowledge, skill, or experience needed, can leave us on the "cliff" of financial anxiety. Or worse, may result in financial calamity.

Of course, if we are lacking, we "should" delegate. But, if we desire *complete* financial freedom, we "must" delegate.

A *true financial steward's* role is to stay skilled and knowledgeable in the primary financial disciplines: taxes, financial and insurance planning, and investment selections and market conditions. The knowledge an advisor possesses is part of the assurance an owner needs.

Knowing the advisor understands these disciplines are good "road signs" toward the STRONG TRUST we need. A strong sense of our *steward's authority* is a step toward *the bridge* to financial peace of mind.

ACCOUNTABILITY

Stewards should be found trustworthy in the "little" things. In other words, we, as owners, should be able to count on our delegate's actions to be clearly defined and consistent with our expectations. We hold them accountable.

Delegation of responsibility to a financial advisor should allow for a trial period. During this time, the steward is accountable to and will train us in their set of *reasonable expectations*; what "road signs" we can expect. This relationship is a key step toward *the bridge* to freedom. Its goal is to develop stronger and stronger trust.

Of course, it is important for us, as owners, to understand in advance what attitude and actions are **reasonable**. What assurances can stewards reasonably deliver on a repeatable basis?

Owners should recognize that certain actions or expectations are controllable, while others are easily disrupted by the uncontrollable. And other expectations are simply **unreasonable**.

Maximum return with no risk is unreasonable. Even modest, inflation-hedging growth requires some "draw down" possibilities. Some risk of loss.

And, as owners, we must remember to look beyond the "bottom line" in reports. Unexpected cash withdrawals, for example, have nothing to do with investment performance but are so easily forgotten "pit stops" on our financial road. If reviews only look at ending account values and do not account for those early withdrawals, uncertainty can creep in.

We must work our plans and make our plans work. Remember, the goal is to have *clear, reasonable expectations* and develop STRONG TRUST.

CLEAR & REASONABLE EXPECTATIONS: **THE ADVISORY AGREEMENT**

When we hire a steward, we should see stated in writing what routine actions or other periodic services they can be expected to deliver. These expectations are stated in the advisory agreement between us and the advisor.

A *true financial steward* will require those who are delegating authority to them to really understand who is responsible for what according to that agreement. Unfortunately, many times there is too much rush to get to the back page and have the agreement signed, thereby sealing the hiring process.

SLOW DOWN. Let's make sure all parties set clearly in their minds who is responsible for what actions and the *reasonable expectations* of the service being hired. Sometimes it is important to this long-term relationship to simply jot down an informal summary, or "bullet list," on a memo pad.

- "I will.....
- "They will..."

Just remember, in highly regulated industries, the formal paperwork is the real boss. But we can use this "bullet list" pad technique to stimulate a conversation, reiterate in simplified terms what actions to expect, and begin to build trust.

CLEAR & REASONABLE EXPECTATIONS: **THE TOOLS & STRATEGIES**

We want to build stronger and stronger trust based upon repeatable fulfillment of reasonable expectations. The advisor will use certain tools, techniques, or strategies to try to deliver on those expectations.

It is okay to ask enough questions to understand what tools and strategies we are trusting even if we don't know how they work. Remember, the goal is "release" of responsibilities and enjoyment of *complete* financial freedom.

CLEAR & REASONABLE EXPECTATIONS:
EXPECTING THE UNEXPECTED

Certain expectations, though clearly discussed and agreed upon up front, are really not controllable. The biggest of these is what we can expect from the investment markets.

This is like a sailing ship's captain trying to predict the wind. While "predicting" the wind is impossible days out, "reading" the wind and "sailing with" the wind is possible. True stewards, like the ship's captain, can "see a change in the wind."

Some investment expectations are like the wind. They will change over time. For example, consider a person who held one-year CDs between 1979 and 1982 paying 7% to 9%. By 2014, things had changed. But their expectation may still have been, "I can buy CDs for safety and income. Right?" Well, the correct expectation from 2013 to 2016 was that one-year CDs would be paying less than 1%.

In other words, expectations should be restrained by understanding limitations and changing market conditions; the "changing winds."

The regulatory authorities call explaining limitations "full disclosure." Sometimes this "full disclosure" can seem to defeat one of our primary purposes, to help the owner have peace of mind. This should not be so. These "disclosures" should be understood as helping to build that sense of *repeatable, reasonable expectations* which will grow STRONG TRUST, SMART CHOICES and help us cross *the bridge* to freedom.

These disclosures admit the inherent uncertainty in investment market expectations and the need for periodic authoritative action based on those "changing winds."

Translation: Disclosures do not do away with uncertainty. They put them in focus. It is easier to address the "focused" problems than those "out of focus." It is easier to work with the "changing wind" than to try to sail against it. Or act like it will never change.

What we owners need is *the steward's assurance* that every effort possible will be made to deal with the uncertainties while planning for the repeatable, reasonable outcomes that are more certain.

<u>An Example of "Full Disclosure"</u>

For example, at Swords Wealth Management, LLC (www.swordswealthmanagement.com), they use a proprietary trend weighting system for preservation or deployment of investment assets. This system is referred to in their advisory agreement and disclosure documents. They will also discuss it in client meetings. This system examines the price trends of numerous investment indices to determine if there is more of a heightened risk or a heightened reward environment. This determination can call for tactical investment changes.

While this proprietary model is constantly evolving, it represents a substantial experiential work that SWM places some degree of trust in for their decision-making on behalf of clients. To the extent that they may discuss this system, they also make disclosures of its inherent weaknesses and risk of sole dependency on this or any other systems exclusively.

They believe the system does work. It is in the best interests of the owners and has helped them to preserve clients' principal in substantial down markets.

Why the disclosures then? It is important to create a reasonable expectation of the manager's capabilities instead of some false hope. Hope, when unrealized, breeds a WEAK TRUST and financial worry. We want to take that critical short step away from this "cliff."

CLEAR & REASONABLE EXPECTATIONS: **CONFIDENCE WITH THE UNCONTROLLABLE**

While the "changing winds" of the investment world may be uncontrollable, the steward's response is controllable. Our financial plans may need adjusting. Our investments may need changing.

The person able to help us do that will sound a certain way. They will sound like someone setting the "plumb lines" of reasonable expectations: Exactly what can be defined; also, what cannot be clearly known in the beginning. These are persons of *steward's authority* and worthy of trust.

When we, as owners, test their knowledge, we should hear facts we could verify. When we hear their stories, we should hear in their voice expectations based on their experience. We should be listening for patterns of actions that lead to positive, repeatable experiences. These set our reasonable expectations; our "road signs" to expect on our financial road, our TRACT of TRUST. This is the gauge of our *steward's authority* and the basis of our step toward *the bridge* to freedom.

We should expect the steward to include the bad news, such as "uncertainty always exists." It does. It is no use pretending that it doesn't. His tools, techniques, and strategies all have limitations. This is just part of the financial and investment planning world. We should be sure to "deposit" these discussions into our confidence base to build a sense of what "changing winds" and responses to reasonably expect. We are building stronger and stronger trust in the *steward's authority* with both what is controllable and what is not.

Saying it again, the goal is "release" of responsibility and enjoyment of *complete* financial freedom by us, the owners.

STRONG TRUST: THROUGH EXPECTATIONS & EXPERIENCES

In summary, through good delegation, stronger and stronger trust is grown by experiencing *clear, reasonable expectations*; walking the TRACK of TRUST with our steward.

In working with a financial steward, we discuss the expectations up front. We, the owners, will use the testing and trial period to gain experience in "riding the changing winds." Trust in our delegate's handling of both the controllable and uncontrollable should grow.

What we want is STRONG TRUST based on repeatable, measurable experiences. To develop STRONG TRUST we need *expectations* that are accurate in the experience of someone who has the true skill to manage responsibilities and is willing to have those expectations tested over time.

We need the help of a person of *steward's authority*; a person of accurate expectations and good experience. In the testing and trial period, we are learning the *steward's authority* and gaining trust in it. We also want to gain confidence in the tools and techniques they use on our behalf.

Through the initial setting of expectations and the testing and trial period, trust should grow as we understand well a number of things:

- What controllable actions our steward may take without consulting us.
- What controllable actions are expected from us in regard to our estimated retirement cash needs?
- What if we have an unexpected, major cash need arise? How will such an uncontrollable requirement for instant "liquidity" be handled?
- What will happen when the uncontrollable investment market trend changes (i.e., the "changing winds")?

- How will the impact of an uncontrollable "bear" market be responded to in our long-term plans?

In addition, owners should set in our minds what additional controllable actions or services will be performed annually, quarterly, or at some other increment of time during the relationship. These will become the sign posts on our financial road of trust, our TRACK of TRUST.

Again, this is about building stronger and stronger trust in *clear, reasonable expectations.* It will be rewarded with financial peace of mind. We are stepping away from the "cliff" and toward *the bridge.*

Ben's Response:

In our initial financial road map discussions, we have to start with where the client is now. We task our clients with bringing in their investment statements, tax returns, and Social Security benefit documents to determine their starting point in valuable assets and income.

We have found that the mere exercise of gathering these documents actually begins the process of delegation and financial freedom for our clients. It is in this personal "accounting" that we begin to recognize clients moving toward stronger trust in us. And then as we talk through reasonable expectations, that begins to instill our objective: STRONGER TRUST, SMARTER CHOICES, and financial peace of mind.

Steve: On the Delegate and Release FREEDOM

A large part of financial worry comes from what we call the *delegate and release PROBLEM* of "blind faith." Many advisers would like us to simply have "blind faith" in their services.

No questions. No expectations. No accountability.

As we stated in Chapter 4, an emotional "cliff" between us and financial peace of mind is "poor delegation..." based on WEAK TRUST and its relative, "blind faith." Whether we like it or not, financial anxiety will not go away without trust and discipline. "Blind faith" is not this discipline.

"Blind faith" is acting without accountability and with a lack of *clearly defined* and *reasonable expectations* that can be quantified and trusted.

Remember, "blind faith" is acting on WEAK TRUST or "just because." It is acting on what may be unproven, unrepeatable, or untrustworthy. A lot of *financial worry* rests in this fog around the cliff. Let's clear the fog that causes such poor choices.

SMART CHOICES IN THE TRUSTWORTHY

If "blind faith" is acting on the untrustworthy, then a good action would be making SMART CHOICES on the trustworthy. The trustworthy are those repeatable, measurable experiences we can count on. The basis for developing stronger and stronger trust is making SMART CHOICES, educated decisions to act on what can be trusted.

What can be trusted and, therefore, is a SMART CHOICE in the financial services world?

Previous experiences should lead future expectations. This is why we want our steward to be a person of good experience.

The smart money makes decisions based on experience and *clear, reasonable expectations* in regard to finances. These expectations are those that can be quantified, measured, and, when accounted for, tend to be repeated.

THE *STEWARD'S AUTHORITY* AND EXPERIENCES

While the uncontrollable "changing winds" of our financial world are disruptive, a steward of skill can quantify, measure, and adapt to the change in direction. When tested over time, the *steward's authority* experienced in these matters should impact our convictions. It becomes the foundation of our confidence.

Every *true financial steward* will possess the *steward's authority* to "paint" expectations in the owner's mind and breed confidence in our hearts. It is part of the *steward's assurance*; authority in their voice.

While they must possess skill to "reposition" our financial assets, it is much more important that they possess skill with valuable experiences.

What has dealing with both the controllable and the uncontrollable taught them? Do they have an appropriate response to disruptions in their otherwise controllable expectations?

This experience is the basis of the authority in their voice.

In the beginning of our relationship with them, there is nothing wrong with the owner "borrowing" their *steward's authority*. But we need our trust to grow through experiencing their skills.

Remember, the goal is "release" of responsibility and enjoyment of peace of mind and *complete* freedom. This comes through STRONG TRUST and SMART CHOICES based in part on the *steward's authority*.

STRONG TRUST, SMART CHOICES

In financial services, trust and confidence in our decision to fully release responsibilities is strengthened by a set of trustworthy experiences. Whether we "borrow" experiences from our *steward's authority*, or from other's experiences, we should be building toward STRONG TRUST and confidence. We want that certain settling feeling we can't quite explain that lets us sleep peacefully at night.

We know our steward is a person "having authority." This is the source of our financial peace of mind. We are beginning to cross over *the bridge*, over our *chasm of concerns*.

We are approaching *complete* financial freedom.

For example, consider the parable of a very intelligent, elderly widow who complained of stomach ulcers caused by financial worry. With the help of a steward, she develops a sound financial and investment plan based on a very clear set of expectations. Further, she hires the steward to help her fulfill those expectations with diligence and focus. She begins to experience much more than financial peace of mind.

Two years go by and she is found not only grateful at the trustworthiness of her steward, but reporting that her stomach problems had disappeared.

A person like this would have developed STRONG TRUST. Financially, she would have become more "secure." This is what *complete* financial freedom looks like.

If we have STRONG TRUST and make SMART CHOICES using the *steward's authority,* we are developing more confidence to "release" responsibility for wealth and enjoy that freedom.

Ben's Response:

Remember my reference in the last chapter to the Y2K phenomenon of the late 1990s? At a previous firm, I was tasked with preparing our firm's computers for the new millennium. As I called around to other professional firms, I quickly learned that many businesses were not doing any planning at all.

But we wanted STRONG TRUST.

We conscientiously worked out a plan that would give us *clear, reasonable expectations* of what would happen when the date turned to the year 2000. We leaned heavily on a borrowed set of experiences others previously had and we set our STRONG TRUST, our reasonable expectations.

We also planned to monitor the situation and respond accordingly if our reasonable expectations were not met.

In this case we did not rely on blind faith that our computers would be sound but instead we had contingency plans. The confidence this thorough approach gave us created in us STRONG TRUST that the outcome would be positive.

And it was! We reinforced our set of experiences into a STRONGER TRUST and SMARTER CHOICES and set the stage for a confident approach in faith to handle the next similar situation to occur.

We plan our work, work our plan. We monitor our plan, adjust if needed, and go forward with confidence.

>> CHAPTER 6

WHAT KIND OF SERVANT TRULY *DELIVERS* FREEDOM?

Who then is the faithful and sensible slave whom his master put in charge of his household to give them their food at the proper time? "Blessed is that slave whom his master <u>finds so doing</u> when he comes. Truly I say to you that he will put him in charge of all his possessions.

– MATTHEW 24:45-47

An investment in knowledge pays the best interest.

– BENJAMIN FRANKLIN

Bondservants, be obedient to those who are your masters ...in sincerity of heart, as to Christ....

– EPHESIANS 6:5-7

\>> ALL CHRISTIANS ARE CALLED TO WORK AS IF FOR THE LORD ON EARTH

\>> "BONDSERVANT":

- "ONE DEVOTED TO ANOTHER IN DISREGARD OF HIS OWN INTERESTS."

\>> A FEW WELL THOUGHT OUT QUESTIONS CAN SCREEN OUT INEXPERIENCE

Steve's Story: "Bondservants" Who Work as to Christ *Deliver*

The proposition of the first few chapters is big. A person or family of wealth can entrust their resources to certain individuals who can be counted on to "deliver" highly responsible management. When they are delegated this authority, the owner can completely release concerns about wealth management. The owner simply directs what they want and the servant delivers.

What kind of advisor will really do this? Once we have found a prospective steward, how do we know if they will be highly responsible with our resources? How do we know we can "release" wealth responsibilities into their care?

These are excellent questions and one which every owner should seek to get answered.

I had been a highly responsible steward and I wanted someone like me to partner with my wife and me in handling our wealth responsibilities. My desire was to serve God by serving my clients. Actually, all Christians are called to work as if for the Lord on earth.

> "Whatever you do in word and deed, DO ALL in the name of the Lord Jesus...." (Colossians 3:17)

Another Bible verse says:

> "Bondservants, be obedient to those who are your masters according to the flesh, with fear and trembling, in sincerity of heart, AS TO CHRIST; not with eyeservice, as men-pleasers, but as bondservants of Christ, doing the will

of God from the heart, with goodwill doing service, as to the Lord, and not to men...." (Ephesians 6:5-7)

During my working years, these scriptures guided me not to merely look around for the "norm" of service, but to offer a higher caliber of service. I called this *world class service.*

I had been willing to do it. I knew there were others willing to do the same. It involved doing the will of God while trying to do what the client wanted. It involved using my knowledge, skill, and experience to serve the client's needs "in sincerity of heart...as to the Lord and not to men...."

When it was time to release the responsibilities of my personal wealth management to another, this is the attitude I was looking for. When I engaged Ben as a steward for my wife and me, we tested his attitudes by observing his actions. We found him to be a person of knowledge, skill, and integrity as well as being a Christian.

He serves us well.

Ben's Response:

I remember Steve talking about bondservants as mentioned in the Bible. The biblical definition of a bondservant is one devoted to another in disregard of his own interests. In other words, if the owner was away, a household bondservant would be entrusted to run the house just like the owner. The servant learns the values and goals unique to the owner.

Just like those "bondservants" of those households they served, we attempt in all ways to be found faithful and sensible in focusing on those values and goals of the households we serve.

We view our role as a trust. If perils come, we are prepared and we deal with it. If opportunities present themselves, we try to take advantage of them. Just like the owner.

A large segment of our clients are children of the "greatest generation." Their parents struggled through depressions and world wars and built modern-day America. These parents taught that sacrifice and thrift were important. They helped forge the economy that has helped create the American Dream for so many over the last century. Those seizing the opportunities created new millions in accumulated wealth.

To serve this generation is an honor and a responsibility that is uniquely satisfying.

We want those we serve to enjoy financial peace of mind knowing someone of authority can be counted on to help them manage, during more difficult times, the wealth they earned.

Steve: On Defining "Financial Steward"

If we use the biblical definition of a manager or steward, we will find a word for *household servant* that the owner of the house trusts.

As Ben mentioned above, the word in the original Greek language translates as "bondservant":

- "One who gives himself up to another's will....," or
- "One devoted to another in disregard of his own interests."

I like to use golf analogies because I play often. Also, golf is a game of rules and integrity as well as requiring practice to develop skill.

UTMOST INTEGRITY

In the bible story the high trust by the owner implies that this "bondservant," or steward, is a person of utmost integrity.

The person of utmost integrity is not a person who in playing golf bends the rules when they need to for his or her own selfish gain. This person's ball comes to rest just out of bounds but they think no one sees it but them. A little "foot wedge" and they're back in play, at least in their mind. This is not integrity.

Integrity does the right things even if no one is looking.

SKILL

A steward is a person of skill.

It is one thing to play golf. It is another thing to be skilled at it through discipline and practice. A golfer of skill will be apparent in their swing and in their average score over time. Their "handicap," as golfer's call their skill gauge, becomes lower as more and more skill is developed.

In financial and investment planning, the person of skill will have tools and processes in place that demonstrate a professionalism. They will have a history of utilizing those tools to make better and better decisions to preserve and grow wealth over the long term. When they describe what to expect, they are accurate more often than not. We can count on their developed skills.

KNOWLEDGE & COMPLIANCE

A steward is a person of knowledge and compliance.

There are professional designations or registrations that can give us some degree of comfort in this area:

- CFP®s - Certified Financial Planners must stay in good standing with annual continuing education.

  In addition, they must abide by a Code of Ethics and Rules of Conduct. These Rules of Conduct actually require the professional to put their clients' interests ahead of their own at all times.
- CPAs - Certified Public Accountants must stay in good standing and meet annual continuing education and periodic ethics requirements.

- *A Registered Investment Adviser* is either state or federally registered with securities boards and must maintain certain policies, procedures, and ethical standards above and beyond the normal "broker."

EXPERIENCE WITH ISSUES OF LIFE: THE "CLIFFS"

A steward is a person of experience with the issues of life the owner faces.

There is no substitute for time and hands-on experiential knowledge through several market cycles and with many different household scenarios. As owners, we have unique emotional as well as financial issues that impact our decisions.

Do we really want someone working for us who has never had practice applying the tax laws? Do we want someone without experience using the many types of investments? Do they have experience with the substantial damage lurking in "bear markets"?

Do we really want someone serving us who either doesn't want to or can't tell us what tendencies wage-earners or retirees may have that would be a cliff of devastation to our financial plans?

The *chasm of chaos* has many cliffs in addition to those mentioned in Chapter 4. Some are emotional. Some are financial. Don't we want our delegate to have a working knowledge and experience with these?

A few well thought out questions can screen out inexperience that can cost us thousands of dollars. Such as: "When was the last bear market?" And, "Assume I was a client of yours during that time. What actions, if any, did you take on my behalf? What defensive transactions showed up on my statements?"

These are good questions. We want to know if they have a strategy planned to defend our wealth in treacherous markets.

Does the person have good experience? Experience that he learned from? Or is it merely years of experiences without learning; bad experiences, repeated over and over, that do no good for the unsuspecting and inexperienced client?

SERVANT-HEARTED & CONSCIENTIOUS

A steward is servant-hearted and conscientious.

The Bible teaches us that the greatest among us must desire to truly SERVE. It also counsels that anyone who would be raised up as a leader should first humble themselves and serve. (Matthew 23:11-12; Mark 10:44). Unscheduled deeds of service and acts of conscience are a great gauge of a steward who can truly help us reach our goals.

For example, who picks up the trash of others on the golf course or in a parking lot? Who returns a golf club to the rightful owner when found out on the course?

The servant who will deliver in time of need, with a conscience, is the one who has such a heart. We call this "sincerity of heart."

Ben's Response:

Certified Financial Planners have to meet a certain set of ethical and practice conduct standards as part of our ongoing licensing requirements. CFP®s must provide their financial planning services as a fiduciary. That is, they must act in the best interest of their financial planning clients. This is part of the *true financial steward* screen.

As such, the CFP® designation is a good standard to use when searching for highly responsible financial advisors.

Advisors who take inappropriate actions for otherwise trusting clients are often caught in violation of certain securities laws and regulations. If you want to check the background of compliance of a certain advisor, these websites are helpful: www.brokercheck.org or www.cfpboard.org.

Persons inquiring will find that we interpret working as unto the Lord as being "above reproach" with regard to complying with industry standards and objectives.

Steve: On the Interview and Trial Period: Testing *High Responsibility*

There are regulators over all high trust professions such as our legal, medical, and banking industries as well as financial planning, investment securities, and investment advisory services. The phrase "holding out" is often used to reference how a broker, agent, accountant, attorney, or financial advisor holds themselves out to the public. How do they market themselves and their services?

At Swords Wealth Management, LLC [www.swordswealthmanagement.com], they hold themselves out to be fiduciaries; what they call *financial stewards*.

In other words, it is always about devotion "to another's will":

- Another's values,
- Another's money, and
- Another's goals that require money.

In many industries, such as that of *registered investment advisers*, regulators will not allow the use of published client testimonials in advertising materials or other marketing efforts.

How is a person to know if their prospective advisor is a highly responsible person in an industry where published testimonials are not allowed?

First, we ask the advisor if we can speak directly with two or three of their clients.

Second, the *interview and trial period* becomes the period to sense the authority the advisor exercises, to discern their servant-heart, and to learn trust. This season of the relationship should be anticipated by all good advisors. It is important to see if what a person or business is holding themselves out to be is accurate. Of course, no true steward would oppose this.

We want to know, "Will this person be a highly responsible person"? The emphasis here will be using the testing and trial period and the set of *clear, reasonable expectations* set forth in our bullet point list. We should use our understanding of the scope of their services to require accountability to a set of reasonable expectations.

It is essential that they not only help us to set in our minds clear expectations, but those expectations be repeatable and measurable so that we can discern their *steward's authority* in carrying out their delegated responsibilities. Remember, the highly responsible person is proving themselves in the "little" things.

EXPECT GROWING TRUST: "LITTLE BY LITTLE"

Trust is not instantaneous. But the trust required for *complete* financial freedom is not a WEAK TRUST either.

While we never should make partner decisions in "blind faith," choosing a financial partner for a lifetime has to start with the first date, so to speak. Hopefully, you have been able to borrow trust in the prospective advisor. Whether through our own discernment or depending on the trust other clients have in an advisor, it is okay to engage with little trust. But quickly expect personal trust to start growing.

True financial stewards will want this in the relationship between the owner and themselves.

There is a wisdom scripture in Proverbs 13 that says:

> "Money that comes easily disappears quickly, but money that is gathered little by little will grow." (Proverbs 13:11 NCV)

Trust is the same way. A *true financial steward* will want a long-term engagement focused on clear and measurable expectations and the opportunity to grow stronger trust little by little. They will welcome the testing and trial period. Their heart is to be proved trustworthy.

My goal during my trial period with Ben was to trust in his knowledge, skill and experience. I wanted a sense of his *steward's authority* when it came to matters of wealth management. But I also wanted my trust to grow and I needed to see that he was servant-hearted.

Ben proved to be much like me. Because he had a heart to serve as well as knowledge and skill, he had developed what it took to be faithful and wise with my personal wealth and to help my wife and me grow our trust. He began to paint expectations in our minds. We began to experience those expectations come true as circumstances unfolded.

When an advisor does this for the owners, it makes for stronger and stronger trust and the feeling we are making smarter choices. This is what we need for financial peace of mind and financial freedom.

Steve: The Christian Screen: Testing *Sincerity* of Heart

I heard a minister tell a story one time about sincerity. He told us that the word "sincere" literally means "without wax." The word comes from a story of old world sculptors and the extreme effort made to value their work. When a piece of sculpted art was done correctly it could be invaluable.

Unfortunately, the art of sculpting stone involves much skill. Some unscrupulous men in the effort to hide their lack of skill would fill in their cracked stonework with wax. While not easily seen by the normal art lover, experts in the field would know to hold the work up to the light. This was a test. While the light would not shine through the stone, it would instantly reveal the application of wax to a crack and the dishonest attempt to hide flaws.

The most valuable pieces were said to be "without wax." When we think of "sincere," we should think of things that are without flaw when exposed to light. So it is that Christians believe in a conscience that is good before Christ, the true Light of the world. Literally, a "sincere heart" is a heart "without wax," without flaw. A heart not degraded by dishonest intent.

Some men or women will put fish on their business cards or peace symbols on their truck only to be found untrustworthy or flawed by experience. In a world of blatant deception, someone calling themselves "Christian" may indeed be using Christianity more as a marketing gimmick than an indication of the quality of their service.

"Christian" simply means followers of Christ. While none of us are perfect, true Christians should be trying to "maintain a blameless conscience" (Acts 24:16). They are trying to be mature in biblical principles (Hebrews 6:1).

A true Christian should make a wonderful financial steward. They should be servant-hearted and trustworthy. It may help to review some foundational principles of a true follower of Christ. These should guide our discernment in choosing a "Christian" as our steward.

The following questions are a good preliminary screen to test the "sincerity of heart" or genuine nature of those who offer their services:

- Do they treat Jesus Christ as Lord-leader of their life? Not just "savior," but actually Lord? [see Romans 10:8-12]
- Do they have a regular prayer life of seeking to be led of the Holy Spirit of the Holy Bible? [see Matthew 26:41 and Romans 8:14, 26]
- Do they honor their mother and father? [see Ephesians 6:2-3 for guidance here]
- Do they recognize other authorities God has placed in their lives? [see 1 Peter 2:13-15 for wisdom in this regard]
- Do they have a Christian fellowship or church they regularly attend? [see Hebrews 10:24-25 for more information]
- Are they accountable to Christian church leaders? [see 1 Peter 5:5, Hebrews 13:17 and Ephesians 5:21 for guidance]
- Do they obey the simplest of laws subjecting themselves voluntarily to local, regional, and national laws recognizing authorities as agents of God's good in the earth? [see Romans 13:1-6]

If we can't discern whether a financial advisor meets these criteria, we should ask them outright. If that doesn't work and being a "Christian" is a deal-breaker for us, then look elsewhere. Don't trust them to manage anything.

And even if a prospective steward does meet the criteria of a "Christian," the use of the testing and trial period to let them prove themselves highly responsible advisors is still a key step toward *the bridge* to our *complete* financial freedom.

Ben's Response:

Sometimes the "Christian" screen can become very simple; the advisor seems resistant to answer. More often than not, such resistance to these questions is probably an answer in and of itself. The answer is, "No." Accept it and move on to interview other "Christian" candidates.

The process of engaging a highly responsible person could also include using a designed questionnaire. I suggest a search of www.letsmakeaplan.org. There you will find a questionnaire called, "Ten Key Questions to Ask Your CFP® Professional." You can use these questions to guide you with any potential *true financial steward,* not just Certified Financial Planners.

THE HEARING TEST

Further, I suggest that in your interview you focus on determining first and foremost whether the advisor will actually **hear** your values; what's really important to you. Highly responsible stewards like those advisors of Swords Wealth Management, LLC will desire to "be obedient to their masters" (Ephesians 6:5-7) so to speak.

During the financial planning process I took Steve and his wife through, we sat down to discuss their financial future. The conversation went well. I was truly trying to **hear** him and his wife. They shared with me their deep core values as well as their retirement goals that required money and some planning.

Later, Steve revealed to me that at this stage of the financial planning process he was still really observing and testing me. He wanted to see what kind of servant I would be. He said something to me that I will never forget.

He said he was paying attention to how much of the time I was talking versus listening. Mentally, he was assessing what he calls the 60/40 gauge: what percentage of the conversation did I listen, really listen, trying to understand his and his wife's feelings. He wanted the conversation to be more of a 60% steward/40% owner mix. While the steward needed to guide the conversation, the owner's thoughts were really what was important.

If I would have talked closer to 80% to 90% of the time, then most likely I was not really **hearing** them. He stated, "Hearing is key to true stewardship on behalf of our owners. Without truly hearing them, how could we really plan properly for them?"

I believe that this is true. If the advisor you are interviewing is not trying to learn your personal situation and understand your values and goals, then, once again, we suggest looking elsewhere.

Steve: On who truly *delivers*...

What kind of a servant is most likely to deliver *complete* financial freedom? A *true financial steward*, a "bondservant" who works as to Christ in sincerity of heart, can deliver freedom.

The TRACK of TRUST laid out by the steward will reflect the directions of the owner, *clear, reasonable expectations* from the steward's experience, the *steward's authority*, and the well-defined plan prepared in conjunction with the steward himself.

We will discuss what constitutes a well-defined plan in the next chapter.

>> CHAPTER 7

THE *WELL-DEFINED* PLAN & THE "DO I HAVE ENOUGH" MODEL

Give me six hours to chop down a tree and
I will spend the first four sharpening the axe.
– ABRAHAM LINCOLN

The goal of retirement is to live off your assets-not on them.
– FRANK EBERHART, Plan Ahead:
Protect Your Estate and Investments

Financial security and independence are like a three-legged stool
resting on savings, insurance and investments.
– BRIAN TRACY, Power of Discipline: 7 Ways It Can Change Your Life
Leading authority on the enhancement of personal effectiveness

By being modest in your spending, you can ensure you will have
enough for retirement and can give back to the community as well.
– DAVE RAMSEY, National best-selling author and
radio host, *America's trusted voice on money*

- >> IF ASKED, I CAN SHOW IT ON A NAPKIN AT THE DINNER TABLE.
- >> THERE ARE SEVERAL THINGS WE NEED TO KNOW TO DETERMINE WHETHER YOU HAVE “ENOUGH”.
- >> IT IS IMPORTANT TO NOT UNDERESTIMATE THE NEED FOR ACCURATE LIFE$TYLE SPENDING DATA AND *SOUND ASSUMPTIONS*.

Steve's Story: 30 Years Summarized on a Napkin

Understanding financial and investment planning should not be that difficult. If asked, I can show it on a napkin at a dinner table. More often than not, I present this on a large marker board in my office. I wanted my steward, Ben, to be empowered in each of these areas.

A *well-defined plan* will include both financial planning as well as investment planning components. I coached Ben by explaining my "napkin" presentation, just like I showed new clients for the last 30 years. The concepts have changed a bit over the years, but the overall idea of broad financial stewardship has remained the same.

I begin by contrasting personal financial planning versus investment planning. I draw a giant "T" on the napkin putting, PFP on the left and IP on the right. See Exhibit 7-1. I explain, "PFP stands for Personal Financial Planning. IP stands for Investment Planning."

I begin by listing the financial planning disciplines on the left side with bullet points somewhat as follows:

- Cash Management (routine and liquidity needs)
- Risk Management (insurable risks)
- Tax Planning (income tax avoidance; estate taxation)
- Estate Transitions (use of account registrations; trusts?)
- Retirement ("enough?")

At this point I draw a horizontal line across the bottom of the napkin and divide it into eight to 10 sections indicating years. This is our planning time horizon and will represent the client's longevity, with the far right side indicated with "H" (see Exhibit 7-1). I explain, "Do you know what 'H' stands for? That's when you go home to be with the Lord."

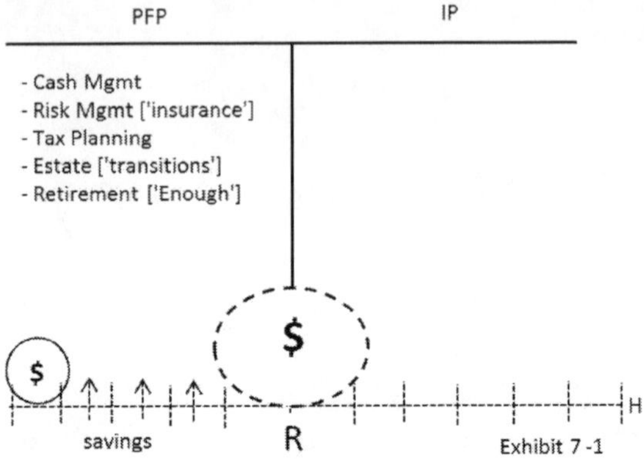

Exhibit 7-1

In approximately the middle of the horizontal line I draw a big circle with a "$" inside of it. "This represents your investment assets you've accumulated so far," I say.

Then I draw an "R" under the time horizon line, leaving a few years to the right of the circle. "This represents your retirement date."

With regard to this left side, the personal financial planning or "PFP" side, the rest of the patter goes something like this:

"There are several things we need to know to determine whether you have 'enough.'

"What will your lifestyle spending be?" (I usually make the S in lifestyle into a $.)

"How much will the cost of living go up by inflation? (After I say that about inflation, I mark each year on the time horizon line, starting at the left side and going all the way to the right, with progressively larger $s indicating rising cost of living. See Exhibit 7-2.)

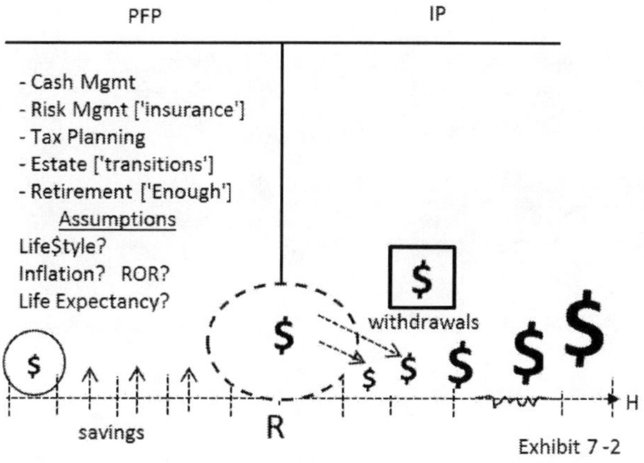

"How much will you save between now and retirement?" (Here I draw an up arrow from each year before, or to the left of, the "R" indicating savings going up into the investment portfolio.)

"What is your life expectancy?" (After asking this I draw a box with a "$" inside and make this statement.) "This is your retirement spending. You need one of these for every year of your life expectancy past retirement; or to the right of this 'R'."

I conclude the left side by explaining that these are the "enough" variables: "The key assumptions of your financial life." Then I ask a very important question: "Can you see how at this point we have not even talked about your investment plans?"

True financial stewards want the perspective financial planning client to recognize that, as servants, they are helping manage so much more than just the investments.

At that point we turn our attention to the right side of the large "T," the investment planning or "IP" side.

We begin to explain: "Most people either want to grow their assets or preserve their assets" (writing on the right side the word "GROW" and "PRESERVE" underneath it. See Exhibit 7-3).

We then simply explain, "Most people who are growing their assets are 'accumulators' (writing that word behind "GROW"). However normally those who retire completely are 'distributors' meaning they are taking cash distributions (writing the word "distributor" behind the word "PRESERVE")."

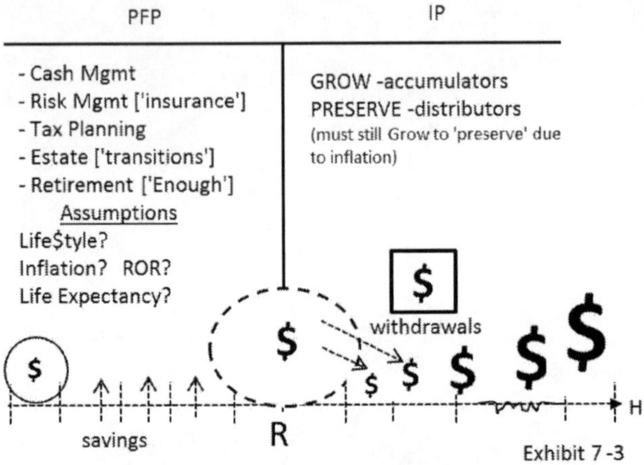

Exhibit 7-3

I then explain that even those who are preservation-oriented need some growth because of the ravages of inflation: "Therefore, even if a person is preservation-focused they need some 'growth'," I say.

Finally, we explain that it is our belief that investments should be partitioned for liquidity at five-year increments of time horizon into their future.

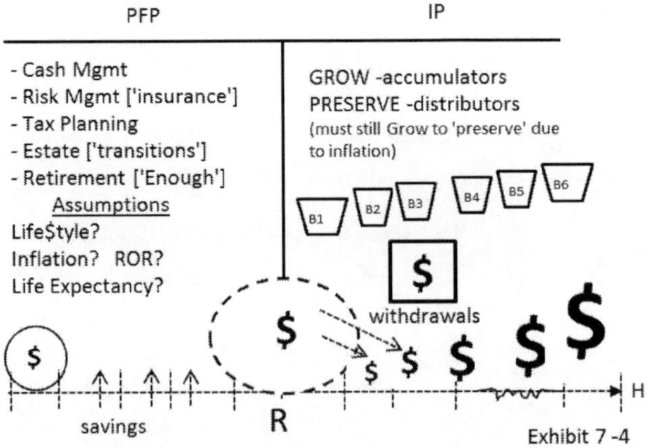

Exhibit 7-4

"We call these baskets of money. Each basket represents incrementally more risk as we allow greater time horizon." (see Exhibit 7-4)

[End of Presentation]

I finished my coaching of Ben by saying, "When we're all done with the napkin approach, the client has a simple but broad layout of what personal financial planning (PFP) and investment planning (IP) components need to be agreed upon. This should become the foundation of the steward's responsibilities. By the time we document all of these elements, we have a thorough, *well-defined plan*."

As a professional CFP® with more than 27 years of experience at that time, Ben agreed.

Most *true financial stewards* will simultaneously build a financial model of data and assumptions that can be accessed by both the owner and the advisor. At Swords Wealth Management, LLC, they use a web-based application providing a portal of access through their website. This model discloses all the assumptions and illustrates how each assumption impacts the owner's long-term expectations. This model can be adjusted and refined at any point in time in the future. They call this the *"Do I have enough?"* planning model.

Ben's Response:

It is important to not underestimate the need for accurate life$tyle spending data and *sound assumptions*. After all, this information will be used to project your long-term cash plans and determine whether you will have enough money for long life.

At times we uncover the stark reality that there is indeed not enough resources for the financial goals. A lot of emotion can be involved. Many times these were "the goals of a lifetime." Almost without exception, such revelation is greeted with new and grateful perspective.

Goals may get reshuffled in terms of spending priority. Values may dictate the desire to eliminate some unreasonable goals.

Though budgeting can sound somewhat dreadful or boring, the process of financial projecting can be very enlightening and a great stress reliever and confidence booster. Remember, the goal is to develop STRONG TRUST in *clear, reasonable expectations.*

And wow. When "goals of a lifetime" are within reach, and the client has *high faith* in those goals being realized, the experience is wonderful.

Either way, the *steward's authority* in financial management, using professional tools and skills and experience, helps promote peace of mind and advances financial freedom.

>> CHAPTER 8

3 SIMPLE STEPS TO MAKE THE PLAN WORK

The beginning is the most important part of the work.
– PLATO (BC 427-BC 347) Greek philosopher.

It is a mistake to look too far ahead. Only one link in
the chain of destiny can be handled at a time.
– WINSTON CHURCHILL (1874-1965) British politician.

Go to the ant, O sluggard, observe her ways and be wise,
Which, having no chief, officer or ruler,
prepares her food in the summer
And gathers her provision in the harvest.
– PROVERBS 6:6-8

Plan your work for today and every day,
then work your plan.
– NORMAN VINCENT PEALE (1898-1993) Protestant preacher and author

>> WE HAVE REAPED THE REWARD OF BEING FOUND FAITHFUL IN THE "LITTLE THINGS" OF MANY. THE PRIZE IS "TRUE RICHES" IN WISDOM, INSIGHT, AND UNDERSTANDING.

>> THERE IS NOTHING WRONG WITH WORKING PART-TIME IN SEMI-RETIREMENT. WE CALL THESE THE "HARVEST WHEN YOU CAN" YEARS.

>> OUR TRUE FINANCIAL STEWARD SHOULD BE SOMEONE OF INTEGRITY DELEGATED TO MANAGE OUR HOUSEHOLD FINANCIAL PLAN. WE SHOULD STAY FOCUSED ON THE DISCIPLINES OF SUCCESS IN OUR INDUSTRY DURING OUR PRE-RETIREMENT YEARS.

Steve's Story: "The 50 Masters": the Reaping of "True Riches"

As of several years ago, I estimated that I had retired through the lives of more than 50 clients. Having the fortunate experience of retiring with them and many, many times since then, I developed a true sense of expectations of what it takes to retire successfully.

Now, at Swords Wealth Management, LLC, the firm I founded, they consider themselves stewards. It is as though they are serving many masters. In coaching Ben, we call those first 50 clients who retired successfully "the 50 masters."

They shared with us their deep core *life values*. They challenged us to help them achieve those core values while planning for and meeting ambitious goals that required money and planning.

The firm gained invaluable experience and honed the knowledge and skills of a *true financial steward* in the process. Its current practice procedures were crafted from those experiences. The practice reaped the reward of being found faithful in the "little things" of many: the prize of "true riches" in wisdom, insight, and understanding. At Swords Wealth Management, LLC, they know how to help owners work their plans.

Steve: On How to *Work* the Plan

STEP#1: HARVEST WHEN CAN: SAVE DILIGENTLY

RECOGNIZE OURSELVES, THE PRE-RETIRED OR SEMI-RETIRED OWNER

When we are a pre-retired owner, we have special considerations for our earnings years prior to retirement. Saving is putting off consuming into the future. We need to determine how many years we have left to work and save like that. Also, what will be our savings rate? How much we can save annually? Referring to our napkin presentation, this is the "send up savings" component. Annual savings are the up arrows; savings ***go up*** into our investment portfolio.

It is correct that saving rates vary for each of us based upon our ability to control our current, pre-retirement life$tyle in exchange for a better, future life$style.

This savings usually involves diligent working years and thrift. It is good to work hard, earning more and saving for tomorrow.

This wisdom scripture guides us in setting back a portion of our income during our earning years:

> "Go to the ant, O sluggard, observe her ways and be wise, which, having no chief, officer or ruler, prepares her food in the summer and gathers her provision in the harvest." – Proverbs 6:6-8

Interpretation: Save for retirement during the harvest season because the winter season will come.

The key in the pre-retirement years is for the owner to begin saving as early in life as possible and to put that savings to work. The sooner we put the savings to work, the sooner the "savings working" will begin to replace "us working."

The true definition of *financial independence* is when our savings is working harder than we are. The closer we get to full retirement, the more this should be true.

Many of us, either through necessity or inspiration, will find ourselves working in our senior years. It is good to make ourselves available to serve where needed and continue to pay for some or all of our life$tyle from our income rather than our savings. There is nothing wrong with working part-time in semi-retirement. We call these the "harvest when you can" years.

STEP#2: MANAGE THE PLAN

CONSIDER A STEWARD AS PLAN MANAGER DURING WORKING YEARS

Another wisdom scripture guides us in consistent, diligent work as a key to long-term financial success:

> "How long will you lie down, O sluggard? When will you arise from your sleep?
>
> 'A little sleep, a little slumber, A little folding of the hands to rest"– Your poverty will come in like a vagabond <u>And your need</u> like an armed man.'" – Proverbs 6:9-11

Interpretation: Wake up, rise up, and find someone to serve with work to avoid being "needy" or living in poverty.

If someone is currently unemployed, find someone to serve and "arise."

If someone already has gifts or knowledge and skills in a certain discipline, try to stay focused.

If someone is a surgeon, he or she should first focus on being the best they can be as a surgeon. If someone is an airline pilot, he or she should focus on being the best pilot possible. If someone owns a manufacturing business, he or she should focus on understanding who they serve and supplying their needs.

There is a greater need for delegating important financial management matters during the pre-retirement years than any other.

For example, if an owner is so busy with his manufacturing business, it would not be uncommon for him and his wife to meet with their steward in which the meeting was predominantly focused on the owner's progress with their plans:

"OK, remind me of my plans," he might say. And, "Am I on track working my plan?"

- "Am I on track with my savings?"
- "Should I use personal as well as employer retirement savings accounts?"
- "Are my strategies for rental properties thought through?"
- "What did we assume in regards to....?" And that's the way the conversation might go.

Our *true financial steward* should be someone of integrity delegated to manage our household financial plan. We should stay focused on the disciplines of success in our industry during our pre-retirement years. The payoff will be greater household earnings and the opportunity to save earlier and more.

"Defend my plan"

Also remember, a big "cliff" blocking our financial peace of mind is spending too much or worrying too much. This results from failure to use good lifestyle estimates. We can STEP BACK and STEP AROUND this cliff and toward *the bridge* to financial peace of mind by asking our steward to defend our plan.

Volunteer to be accountable to the steward to restrain life$tyle, control spending, and stop worrying. Either save now if in the "harvest years" or be willing to spend savings as planned in the retirement years with freedom and peace of mind.

"Help me with my business plans"

Planning may also involve commitment of cash resources toward growing a small to medium-sized business. These business entrepreneurs should consider using a *true financial steward* to help think through personal cash injections or withdrawal strategies and timing. While this involves many other business considerations, our steward makes an excellent partner in considering how business decisions will impact our personal level, household financial planning.

Ben's Response to Step #2:

We store data in a comprehensive financial planning model for each household we serve. It helps us to manage the *complexities* of the many assumptions.

Some of those assumptions should be modified as a person nears retirement age or if the owner simply wants to reduce investment risk.

It is also important to have at least a semi-annual *progress review* in which, among other things, we will make sure the client is staying on track with savings and life$tyle spending goals.

We will also update their liquidity requirements, which can have an impact on their investment planning. Planning for *liquidity events*, whether current or future, such as semi-annual shorter "trips" or buying a new car, often brings a sense of accomplishment and a reminder of good things to look forward to as clients go through their financial lives.

Steve: On Continuing to *Work* the Plan

STEP#3: MANAGE LIFE$TYLE

RECOGNIZE OURSELVES, THE RETIRED OWNER

When we are fully retired, either by choice or by energy, our personal discipline should be first, and foremost, to manage our life$tyle.

Our routine life$tyle includes anything that we would spend repeatedly year after year. We focus on such things as monthly expenditures as well as periodic expenditures for clothing, property taxes, insurance, gifts (including Christmas), etc., that we know we would spend every year.

And our major, extraordinary life expenditures (i.e., once every two to five years) will still need some liquidity planning. These include such things as major home improvements, down payments on houses, automobile replacements, major travel, and reserves for emergency expenditures.

THE NEWLY RETIRED LIFE$TYLE

It is easy in those first few years of retirement to get excited and overspend on "the little extras we deserve"; things like extra trips to visit the grandchildren or that RV so we can "see the world." And our emotion urges, "We deserve this!"

But can we afford it from our nest egg? After all, as we enter the "winter season" of our lives, "harvest times" may be over. Our savings, what we call storehouse or "stores," needs to last. And remember, debt is nothing more than long-term consumption in excess of long-term "stores." And debt is a cliff on the chasm of financial concerns that blocks financial peace of mind.

Stewards understand the desire to have a little extra, to "live a little." So we should make sure our plans account for the "extras." All life$tyle and financial goals properly planned for are not conversations to be avoided. Let's talk them out with our steward. We can anticipate and enjoy our spending goals in their proper time. We do that through solid, sound financial plans.

MANAGE WITH SOLID, SOUND ESTIMATES AROUND RESOURCES

The sooner retirement spending plans are **created**, the better. And the sooner they are **solidified** with sound estimates, the more they can be trusted to contribute to financial peace of mind.

A *true financial steward* will help us map out our financial expectations over our remaining life expectancy. Resources should be allocated over those years.

Two dangerous cliffs to our financial peace of mind are haphazard spending or quick and poor financial decisions.

There is no confidence and peace of mind in failing to firmly plan around **the resources we have**. For many retirees, what we have at full retirement is all there is going to be. This will be a combination of income resources, such as Social Security, pension annuities, commodity or property income like oil and gas income or net rental property income, as well as our accumulated wealth.

We believe in trusting the Lord for lasting security. But as we read in the wisdom scripture from the Bible, He guides us to "gather" our "provision in the harvest" because *the winter years* of little or no harvesting will come. For most, these are what we call the "full retirement" years.

To this day my son remembers one of the primary lessons I taught him as a child about money: "You can only spend it once." This is never so true as it is upon our full retirement. We must manage around our resources as they exist.

A WORD ABOUT DEBT

In our current social culture, credit cards and other installment debt can help us manage cash flow. But in no way should these debt instruments be used to cover or pay for our life$tyle. To do so is to incur *ugly debt*.

We recognize *ugly debt* because its providers demand immediate payment, usurious fees, or our hard labor for money previously enjoyed. We feel pressure to repay them quickly.

If we wouldn't use our limited and precious resources to buy something in cash, we probably shouldn't buy it on credit.

Sometimes the use of credit cards is so easy, we end up spending much more than we mean to. We should ask ourselves this key question: "Do I know how much money I spent on credit cards in the last three to four weeks?" If we don't, look out. *Ugly debt* is lurking.

Smart retirees avoid *ugly debt* unless they plan to go back to work. Do we really want to go back to work? After the years of "us working," we want our accumulated "savings working." It, along with our income subsidies while they last, should provide all our spending power in retirement.

A WORD ABOUT THE MENTAL TRANSITION INTO RETIREMENT

Mentally, retirees must make the transition from **net earners** to **net consumers**.

When we were a **net earner**, we were earning more than we spent; even saving. Or we could earn that "little extra income" for those "little extra expenses" when we wanted to.

Net consumers typically are spending more than their income. This is perfectly normal in retirement. But most likely, the "extra" earned income and savings years have ended when "us working" stops.

If our accumulated wealth is insufficient to meet our desired retirement spending, savings accounts will dwindle too fast. When we wake up to the fact that we can't or don't want to work for that "little extra" anymore, our financial security is challenged.

Many times, an owner will think that the best solution is simply to accept more investment risk, targeting higher investment returns to compensate. Unfortunately, this is not a solution that promotes financial peace of mind.

During the years of "us working," a little extra earned income could provide for "the little extras." During the full retirement "savings working" years, when we want our accumulated savings to last for a lifetime, more caution in spending should be taken. As hard as it may seem to adjust life$tyle downward, it has a more peaceful resolve than does the alternative.

Life$tyle planning should really include assumptions about "the little extras." In addition, an effort should be made to anticipate all major spending, even if one time or nonrecurring – things like replacement of air conditioning units, inside and out, a new roof, or that "bucket list" trip of a lifetime.

When smart planning shows that current life$tyle and these liquidity events and the "little extras" are all well within reach, financial peace of mind rises.

Plans will work if we work plans with these basics in mind.

>> CHAPTER 9

5 BASICS OF SMART INVESTMENT PLANNING

When it comes to the world of investing,
three words come to mind:
overwhelming, intimidating, and scary.
For us "regular Joes," the questions seem never-ending.
– DAVID BAKKE, contributing author, Investopedia

The beginning of wisdom is: Acquire wisdom;
And with all your acquiring, get understanding.
– PROVERBS 4:7

The individual investor should act consistently
as an investor and not as a speculator.
– BEN GRAHAM (1894-1976) Known as
"the father of value investing" and the "Dean of Wall Street"

>> THIS "GOOD OLE BOY" MIGHT SAY TO AN ADVISOR, "WELL, IT IS REALLY SIMPLE. I WANT MAXIMUM RETURN WITH NO RISK."

>> AS YIELD ON INVESTMENTS DECLINED, IT USHERED IN A GREATER NEED TO DISCERN THE TREND IN PRICE CHANGES; WHETHER PRICE TRENDS WERE UP OR DOWN.

>> MOST LAY INVESTORS ARE LITTLE INCLINED TO DEAL WITH THE EMOTIONAL ASPECTS OF INVESTING AND OFTEN SELL AT THE EXACT WRONG TIME OR NEVER SELL AT ALL.

Steve's Story: The "Good Ole Boy" Wants Maximum Return and No Risk

Today, the advisors of Swords Wealth Management, LLC start most new client investment planning meetings by showing a risk versus return "L" chart. This chart has greater return from low to high on the left, vertical axis and indicates increasing risk on the horizontal axis from left to right. Simply put, any spot on the chart will show a tradeoff of increasing risk along with increasing returns. See Exhibit 9-1.

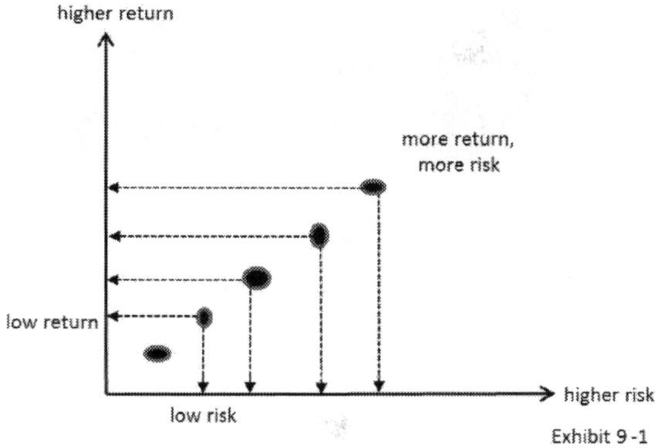

Exhibit 9-1

Imagine the "good ole boy" story. You know who the "good ole boy" is, don't you? That's the person everybody loves because he tries to keep everything very, very simple.

This "good ole boy" might say to an advisor, "Well, it is really simple. I want maximum return with no risk."

On a risk return chart, he would want maximum return on the vertical axis and barely any risk showing on the horizontal axis. See Exhibit 9-2.

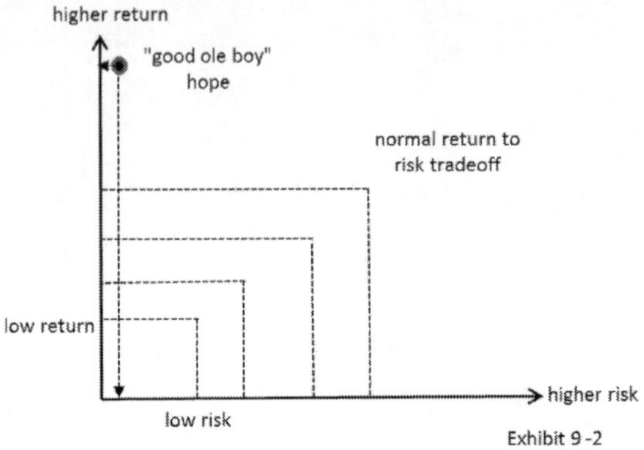

Exhibit 9 -2

Wouldn't we all love that outcome? But unfortunately, it is not a reasonable expectation.

Steve: On Investment Planning's 5 Basics:

Smart investment planning can be broken into five basic concepts:

1) Understanding how *desired investment risk* may differ between accumulators and distributors.
2) Understanding the impact of inflation possibilities on the *desired investment risk.*
3) Understanding the calculation of *total return* and its impact on investment decision-making.
4) Understanding historical returns and risk and their related risk/return targets.
5) Understanding *time horizon investing* considering cash needs and liquidity events.

BASIC #1: ACCUMULATORS' vs. DISTRIBUTORS' RISK

One of the first things that must be decided in determining investment appropriateness is to discern whether an investor is an *Accumulator* or a *Distributor*.

Once an investor has entered the stage where they need to take cash distributions or *take down withdrawals* routinely from their portfolio, investment assets may need lower risk and more liquidity. These are *Distributor* investors.

These investors must either have investments paying a high yield (i.e., dividends or interest) or they must routinely be selling off part of their portfolio. The object will be to avoid selling investments going through market price downturns [i.e., "selling low"] or trying to sell investments that otherwise have limited marketability [i.e., investments with limited demand, such as some alternative investments or thinly traded stocks or bonds with long-term maturities].

Accumulators are persons who are generally *sending savings up* into their portfolio. For them more illiquidity or market risk may be appropriate. They do not plan to withdraw the funds so there is little need to plan for selling assets in the intermediate term.

This person can afford to take more investment risk because he is less likely to need to sell during an unexpected market downturn.

BASIC #2: DEALING WITH INFLATION RISK

If an investor has higher inflation expectations or concerns, their invested assets may incur purchasing power losses during the holding period. In such situations, it is common to attempt to achieve slightly higher investment returns to offset this loss of purchasing power.

Imagine an empty parking lot in front of a grocery store on **January 1, 2020.** On that day the store manager has a contest giving away **$1,000 worth of groceries**. The groceries are loaded into shopping carts and put into the empty parking lot in front of the store for show and tell. How many baskets will be seen? Many notice that the $1,000 worth of groceries exactly fills **ten shopping carts** that day.

Ten years later on **January 1, 2030**, the same grocery store manager repeats the contest, giving away **$1,000 worth of groceries**. As before, the parking lot is emptied except for the groceries loaded into the shopping carts and put on display. How many filled baskets are seen this time? This time, many notice that $1,000 worth of groceries only fills **seven shopping carts.**

What happened? The price of the goods rose so that the quantity of goods was less for the same $1,000. This is real inflation. It is a loss of purchasing power.

If observers had attended both contests 10 years apart, they would notice the **$1,000 prize decreased in quantity**: seven shopping carts instead of ten. It results in a lower quantity of goods for the same money. And that is at only about 3% inflation.

Can you imagine the loss in quantity of goods able to be purchased if inflation went to 8.3%, which it averaged from 1973 to 1983?

BASIC #3: UNDERSTANDING *TOTAL RETURN*

There was a day in which many people did not talk about *total return on investments*. Almost every good investment paid a good yield and that interest or dividend was the focus.

Banks were paying 3% to 4% on money market savings accounts. That was the "yield." CDs were paying 6% to 8% yield. People understood investments in terms of "yield."

What they also understood was that the underlying investment did not change in price. We call that a "fixed" investment. These were nice in an environment paying 4% or 8%.

But in an environment such as 2016 in which yields were less than 0.25% on money market accounts and five year CDs were only paying 1.0%, investors had to look elsewhere for investment returns. They had to begin to look at investment returns differently.

Investors have had to look beyond mere "fixed" investments. We have begun asking ourselves questions like, "Can we invest in something that shows price growth as well as yield giving us our required return needed to live on?" This question is the result of needing to live on 3% to 6%; obviously, more than the 1.0% to 2.0% yields available in safer investments.

Many large pension plans and institutional investment portfolios began shifting away from "fixed" investments in order to achieve what they call higher *total return*.

So investors need to understand *total return*. The calculation of *total return* includes both the "yield" aspect and the "changes in price" aspect of an underlying investment.

Simply put, if something is yielding 2% and its average increase in price over the last five years is 4% per year, then its total return averages 6%. The "total" return is the addition of the yield plus the change in price per year stated as a percent.

It is starting to sound complicated, isn't it? It really isn't complicated.

At Swords Wealth Management, LLC, they want clients to better understand good expectations regarding investment returns. With new clients, they go through a simple comparison discussion that shows the two contributing aspects of *total return* for various investments.

The "Total Return" Calculation Discussion

The discussion usually starts by drawing out something like Exhibit 9-3. Then they fill in the blanks using digits down to 0.25 of a percent, converting taxes and inflation to a decimal percent.

They work down the column; each row added or subtracted from the previous.

		CD	Bonds	Stocks	R. E.
Yield [div or int]		____	____	____	____
Price Change	+/-	____	____	____	____
TOTAL RETURN		____	____	____	____
Taxes	-	____	____	____	____
A/T TOTAL RETURN		____	____	____	____
Inflation	-	____	____	____	____
REAL RETURN		____	____	____	____

Exhibit 9-3

In order to make investments comparable, smart investors understand the two aspects of every investment choice. They ask themselves, "What is the contribution towards *total return* that any investment gets from 'yield' versus potential 'price appreciation?'" Unfortunately, price appreciation can become price declines in down markets. That's why we call it "price change +/-." That is the nature of investments that are not fixed in price.

As yield on investments declined, it ushered in a greater need to discern the trend in "changes in price"; whether price trends were up or down. This aspect of *total return* has a more substantial impact on achieving investment returns than ever. If "the trend was not our friend," it probably resulted in negative total return. That's just a fancy way of saying, "We lost money."

And "real return," which is after taxes and inflation, is a major factor in maintaining long-term standard of living.

BASIC #4: HISTORICAL RETURNS & STANDARD DEVIATIONS

Since 2007, in which yields on "fixed" investments began to decline dramatically, the importance of understanding *historical total returns* as well as *historical risk* escalated substantially.

Fortunately, with the advent of the Internet and online access to historical investment return information, this data has become readily available if we know what we are looking for.

But we must also know what it means.

Normally *historical total returns* are stated in terms of "return on investment" or "performance information". Not so well understood is that *historical risk* represents the volatility above or below that "mean" rate of return, normally stated in terms of statistical standard deviation. So "standard deviation" is just a fancy word for the risk involved.

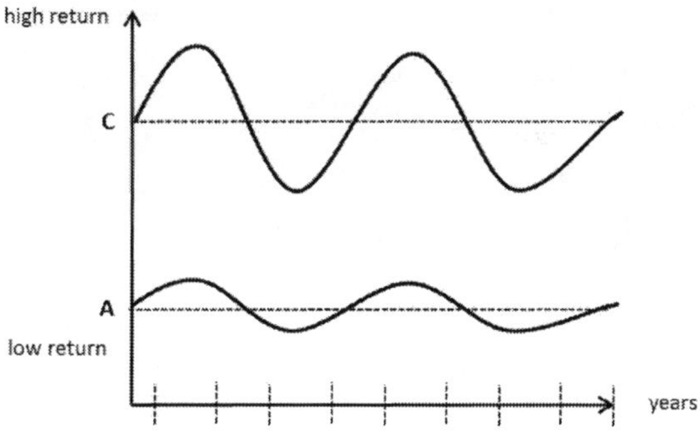

Exhibit 9-4

So while average or "mean" return over the last five years may be represented by a flat horizontal line, as in Exhibit 9-4, the investment performance actually moves along a wavy line. The size of the *swing factor*, up or down, is the size of the risk.

Also, as the chart shows, a span of years is required to achieve the averages or "mean" results (i.e., the flat lines). Any one year taken alone will be an unrealistic picture of what to expect over the longer term.

It is good for the owner to understand these matters. Remember, the goal is to use *clear, reasonable expectations* to reduce the unexpected and its attack on our peace of mind.

And of course, different investments "swing" differently. As illustrated in Exhibit 9-4, investment "A" has lower average return but lower risk. Investment "C" has higher average return but normally higher risk.

When Swords Wealth Management, LLC advisors have this discussion with clients, they will commonly ask, "Which investment do you prefer? Or do you see yourself with a mix of both? Say, a 'B' mix?" [At that they draw in a flat line for "B" between "A" and "C" on the chart.]

The Insecure Investor and Loss of Accumulation Time

Investment decision-makers cannot make smart investment choices without a good expectation of both historical returns and historical risks for various investments. All too often, without reasonable expectations, particularly involving historical risk or downside deviation, an investor can become insecure in the midst of market volatility. They don't know whether this volatility is a normal correction or the beginning of a major trend change.

An **insecure investor** may become too afraid after that swing down to be a buyer or too exuberant after the upswing to be a seller. On the other hand, they may only buy when feeling good about a large upswing or sell when feeling bad about a downswing. Without a *true financial steward* to help them, these emotional investors are being set up for the perfect "buy high, sell low," guaranteed loss scenario.

The buddy on the golf course says, "Wow! Have you seen what the market did the last three months? You better get invested." Interpretation: Your buddy just said, "Buy high." Or worse, the same buddy says, "This market is in crash mode. I'm selling everything and going to cash." Interpretation: Your buddy said, "Sell low."

Ultimately, what we call "the sleep factor" is not so much in the rate of return as it is in how an owner handles this volatility or variation – the "standard deviation" or the *swing factor* away from the normal and expected return in any given year.

This emotional factor should not be underestimated, especially in the hands of the unknowledgeable, unskilled, or inexperienced investors.

It is easy for professionals to say that these down cycles are part of the overall average return on the investment and should be trusted to end; that investments should be "held" through the down swing. Unfortunately, in the last 15 years, we have experienced **two seasons of extended market losses** lasting from nine months to 24 months and devastating trillions of dollars of wealth.

Most lay investors are little inclined to deal with the emotional aspects of investing and often sell at the exact wrong time. When they sell, being afraid, they often do not invest again until many months, sometimes years, after the decline is over. They lose valuable, available returns due to fear.

To never sell can be worse. They don't realize that not only will they lose principal during the down years but now the growth during the recovery years is no new accumulation at all. They are just trying to get back to breakeven. They lose years of accumulation that so many retirement calculator programs assume, incorrectly, to be there.

This is what happens when lay investors are insecure in having no plan for extended down market cycles. We call these extended down trends "bear markets."

Because of this *loss of accumulation time*, in both the actual "bear market" and in the recovery time, "bear markets" can be devastating to a lay investor's long-term financial plans.

A professional financial steward will have a plan of action to attempt to side-step "bear markets." They hope to redeploy with near full original principal when growth markets return, what is now being commonly referred to by market professionals as "risk on." Time should be spent accumulating wealth in good markets, not recovering wealth lost in "bear markets."

We will discuss how to plan for "bear" markets and the need for trend weighting, in addition to good investment selection, in the next chapter.

BASIC #5: TIME HORIZON *BASKET* ALLOCATIONS

The more that we understand how to make cash available strategically at different time periods, the more risk we can take with money not needed during those time periods.

At Swords Wealth Management, LLC, they use the baskets of money allocation system to provide for cash needs based on five-year increments of time.

They attempt to project all routine cash needs (monthly and periodic cash needs during the next 12 months) as well as any event-related cash needs in the next five years (i.e., for things like automobile replacements, travel, home improvements, etc.). Once they have determined these cash needs, they will appropriate funds to cover these future shorter-term needs into a lower risk basket of investments. Let's call this "Basket 1 money."

By definition, that leaves all funds not appropriated for Basket 1 to be invested in longer-time horizon, higher risk, higher return investments.

The premise is that the longer the time horizon, the more risk is appropriate. Conversely, the shorter the time horizon, the less risk is appropriate.

They use a six basket allocation plan.

- Baskets 5 and 6 target 10% or 12% respectively but also rely on the assumption that the investment prices will not deviate more than 20% to 25% off their mean returns of the past 20 years.
- Baskets 3 and 4 target 6% or 8% respectively but also rely on the assumption that the investment prices will not deviate more than 10% to 20% off their mean returns of the past 20 years.
- Baskets 1 and 2 will target investments with lower risk, recognizing that withdrawals will be made from these holdings if withdrawals are needed.

Ben's Response:

As a person gets older, it is common to reduce the investment risk profile. In the multiple baskets of money strategy, reducing investment risk means an allocation that has a lower percentage allocated to basket 5 or 6, the higher risk holdings, and a higher percentage in baskets 2, 3 or 4, the lower risk assets. Plainly, this is just how to make SMART CHOICES.

Steve: On the Big Warning re: "Alternative Investments"

Investments without good *total return* **measurability** have hidden risks. Extra scrutiny should be given before investing in such assets.

Regulators who watchdog over investment securities and investment salespeople have often focused investigations on what they call "alternative investments." These investigations are initiated for two primary reasons:

1) Investment salespeople make large commissions and all too often are found to have sold these investments to those not well suited to invest in them.
2) These investments lack good measurability, having no daily market price.

In addition, these "alternative investments" (sometimes called "Direct Participation Programs") are usually illiquid or nonliquid (i.e., little or no open-market buyers exist) and have an uncertain required holding period. All too often the investment salesman is long gone while the investor is left holding a security with uncertain value and no liquidity.

Unfortunately, the ultimate holding period can vary based on management's discretion. Management's discretion is often not "arms-length" because their management fees continue only if they direct the investment to continue. Even though an **exit strategy** may be anticipated as suggested by the salesman during the initial sales process, the investment sponsor is often earning fees, either directly or indirectly through an affiliate program manager, during any extended holding period.

It was not uncommon for "alternative investments" sold between 1998 and 2008 which anticipated an **exit strategy** within five to seven years, to still be operating in 2015. What investors thought would be a seven-year hold turned into a 10- to 12-year investment.

Part of this extended holding period related to the banking crisis and the "great recession" in 2007-2008. But part was related to management having little incentive to exit.

And keep in mind, return on investment can be reduced substantially from excessive "alternative investment" management fees charged. The combination of underlying asset management fees (i.e., management of real estate assets or equipment leasing assets, etc.), as well as program management fees (i.e., investor services for the "XYZ Partnership Program"), will be collected against the investments' gross revenues. These are often not seen unless special attention is paid to periodic investment reports that disclose them. And all too often these fees are halfway hidden in the endnotes or footnotes.

These investments should only be purchased by those who do not need the money and understand their heightened uncertainties, lack of liquidity or control, and that paying extra fees must require value-added expertise in the proposition.

In the experience of the advisors at Swords Wealth Management, LLC, most of the time the uncertainty and the illiquidity of these investments outweighs the opportunity for higher investment returns.

[i] SEE IMPORTANT ENDNOTE DISCLOSURES

>> CHAPTER 10

4 KEYS TO TACTICAL INVESTMENT CHANGES

Rule No. 1: Never lose money.
Rule No. 2: Never forget Rule No. 1.
– WARREN BUFFETT

Every once in a while, the market does something so stupid it takes your breath away. There are no sure bets in the world of investing; there is risk in everything.
Be prepared for the ups and downs.
– JIM CRAMER, Investor Coach and host of CNBC's "Mad Money"

In the short run, the market is a voting machine, but in the long run it is a weighing machine.
– BEN GRAHAM (1894-1976) Known as "the father of value investing" and the "Dean of Wall Street"

Investing is the intersection of economics and psychology.
– SETH KLARMAN, Margin of Safety:
Risk-Averse Value Investing Strategies for the Thoughtful Investor.

>> WHEN TACTICAL TREND WEIGHTING IS DONE SUCCESSFULLY, MONEY CAN BE REDEPLOYED IN A TIMELY MANNER WHEN GROWTH MARKETS RETURN. THIS ALLOWS MORE TIME SPENT GROWING WEALTH INSTEAD OF MERELY RECOVERING WEALTH.

Steve's Story: The 2000-2002 "Bear Market"

This story could have happened to many advisors after the bear market years of 2000 to 2002. A prospective client comes into their office in mid-2002. Their investment holdings had been more than $700,000 in 1999. They present brokerage statements to prove those values. In June 2002, however, a different set of brokerage statements shows their holdings are now only worth a little more than $400,000 in value.

What had gone wrong?

Without professional supervision, they lacked the discipline and experience to recognize a *major market change* in progress. The failure to monitor and change their investment strategy when conditions warranted such resulted in what we call in Texas "a world of hurt."

It is necessary to understand the importance of price trends in general liquid investments markets. Often by the time a friend or relative mentions the market declines, the busy worker-investor has incurred substantial losses.

A *true financial steward* will have a plan of action to attempt to side step the deep losses of "bear markets." This is called tactical investing. This is not the same thing as some money managers who exercise a high degree of "market timing," which is difficult to do successfully.

When tactical trend weighting is done successfully, money can be redeployed in a timely manner when growth markets return. This allows more time spent growing wealth instead of merely recovering wealth.

In today's chaotic investment world, smart investing will monitor the markets and measure the price action against historical trends. We call this knowing the *price change* trend. As referred to in Exhibit 9-3 of Chapter 9, the + or - of *price change* in any given year is a major portion of *total return* on investment. If the *price change* trend over six to 24 months turns to minuses, we are losing money.

The *true financial steward* will attempt to recognize in advance nonstandard *price change* trends – the potentially devastating, yet developing, "bear market." It is essential to know current *price change* trends and to be able to interpret them against the backdrop of historical norms.

The 4 Keys in Tactical Changes

There are four keys to making tactical investment decisions based on *price change* trends.

1) Understand the importance of *price change* trends in general liquid investment markets.
2) Understand what to do when "the trend is not your friend," the essence of preservation of family wealth.
3) Understand the difference between intermediate to long-term *trend weighting* strategies and short-term "market timing" or "trading."
4) Assuring the decision-maker/steward understands the buy low/sell high requirement for profitable investing.

The ability to interpret and utilize price trend changes could be considered an investment management system. As with any system, it has inherent weaknesses. No one should rely solely on this approach or any other system exclusively.

KEY#1: THE IMPORTANCE OF PRICE CHANGE TRENDS

Good and sensible stewards will use some form of "heat map" to digest tremendous amounts of investment market information and assist them with smart choices. This is simply a color-coded chart of signals (i.e., greens and reds) that indicate key price change transitions. As with any tool, there are inherent weaknesses of such a system and sole dependency on this "heat map" is not responsible stewardship. However, to have no price trend interpretation system at all is to be unprepared.

At Swords Wealth Management, LLC, they have a very defined methodology in place to help them, as stewards for their clients, to distinguish intermediate to long-term *trends* from short-term *noise*.

It may be helpful in understanding trend analysis to discuss how investors have historically evaluated investment opportunities through what is known as "market cycle information."

Market Cycle Information

Investors might make buy or sell decisions based on any or all of the three main types of market cycle information:

A. Cyclical Market cycles: the premise that general economic cycles are dominant in investment risk/reward decisions; phases cycle from recession to trough to growth phase, to peak to recession again.

B. Fundamental cycles: the premise that financial statements and outlook data are dominant in investment risk/reward choices; that individual businesses go through business development cycles that either expand or contract profits that are to be shared with investors and upon which equity prices are determined.

C. Technical cycles: the premise that charting the pattern of *price change* action of traded securities and determining the net buy or sell demand is dominant in investment risk/reward decisions; that indicators such as moving averages and/or other indicators of buyer/seller demand is key in determining *price change* trend.

With the advent of high frequency trading by institutional investors as well as self-direction by the average retail investor, the investors frequently abandon cyclical and fundamental investment research. The investment markets have seemed to diverge from these older, more fundamental forms of decision-making regarding what constitutes an investment opportunity.

Price change trends as seen in technical charting seem to some to be a more accurate indicator of likely future price action. These chart patterns clearly show the net buy or sell demand of investment securities with daily market prices. And this information is readily available to the skilled technician. And when buying demand outweighs selling, early buyers, more likely than not, will see their investment holdings increase in value. When selling demand outweighs buying demand, early sellers may be able to preserve some investment principal.

KEY#2: WHAT TO DO WHEN "THE TREND IS NOT OUR FRIEND"

Financial stewards normally are given decision-making authority on behalf of those they serve. Knowledgeable and experienced advisors will use a combination of subjective as well as non-subjective factors and a decisive model to make SMART CHOICES for clients.

A good decision-maker will know the difference between a clear *price change* trend in a money-making direction, and a clear *price change* trend in a money-losing direction.

In addition, we should not be surprised if at times their analysis helps them see a more uncertain market. We call this an *indeterminate market* with a mixture of *price change* trends. This mixture shows up in a divergence of short-term trends versus longer-term trends, or one investment sector versus another; one a positive *price change* trend, the other a negative *price change* trend.

Most *true financial stewards* are long-term investors. Therefore, they are looking for clear long-term trends in a combination of time horizons. For example, 50-day versus 100-day versus 200- or 250-day trends may be compared.

Indeterminate markets can be sell indicators (i.e., "sell high") if the trend is *a dying bull.* This is when market selling demand over an intermediate term is dominant and clear. In general, this is a money-losing proposition. The "trend is not our friend" as the saying goes.

At Swords Wealth Management, LLC, they use a proprietary *trend weighting strategy.* With it in place, they have a decisive model showing when "the trend is NOT our friend." They most likely will sell positions to preserve principal on behalf of the owners when the SMART CHOICE is no longer to just hold. They believe that under those conditions the owner would more likely lose more and more principal over an uncertain, but extended time horizon.

KEY#3: TREND WEIGHTING IS NOT MARKET TIMING

Market timing has the objective to pick short-term bottoms in order to "buy low" and short term tops in order to "sell high." It attempts to make money in short- to intermediate-term trading, any combination of buying and selling within a shorter-time frame than normal for most investors.

Of course, *market timing* may have its place. A long-term engagement of many *short-term trend trades* can use the volatility of the markets, whether created by business news or world events, to attempt to generate short-term gains over a shorter-term time horizon.

We should consider this speculation. The risk level is very high. And it is very different from what could be called "trend weighting."

At Swords Wealth Management, LLC [www.swordswealthmanagement.com], they consider speculative, higher risk investing, a Basket 5 or 6 risk/reward proposition. They may choose some small allocation to such using well-qualified micro-managers if an owner's risk profile so allows.

Market timing and other trading is not the same as a "trend weighting" strategy. A *trend weighting strategy* does not focus on short to intermediate trends. The core investment philosophy of financial stewards using a *trend weighting strategy* is to be invested in markets with a good money-growing environment over the intermediate to longer term.

As stated before, a *true financial steward* is focused on preserving principal by attempting to sidestep "bear markets." They attempt to redeploy assets when growing markets return. They want invested time to be spent growing wealth, not recovering wealth.

KEY#4: INVESTMENT GAINS: BUY LOW / SELL HIGH

As simple as it may sound to "buy low and sell high," emotions all too often drive investment decisions. This is especially true in the five years from 2011 to 2015 as market volatility reached record levels and market days being up or down 1% to 2% were far more frequent.

As mentioned in Chapter 9 - Basic #4: Historical Returns & Standard Deviations, under the topic "The Insecure Investor," without a smart implementation plan, investors can follow emotions or listen to poor advice and easily make costly "buy high and sell low" mistakes.

A good decision-maker will recognize a clear *price trend* in a money-making direction versus a clear *price trend* in a money-losing direction. However, they may find themselves in an *indeterminate market.*

An *indeterminate market* can be a buying opportunity (i.e., "buy low") if the trend is *a developing bull.* This is not quite a bull market but is moving in that direction. Prices are still relatively low compared to the projection of where they will be as the developing trend continues. In simple terms, this means market buying demand over an intermediate term has been consistent and dominant and worth using as an early indication of a new trend in *price change* that is bullish. In other words, most of the time, this is a money-making proposition.

Smart money people call this a *developing bull.* Experience tells the wise investor that buying in a *developing bull* trend is the best way to buy low in a market seemingly destined to trend higher.

Most of the time, the best buying decisions eliminate emotions and buy not too long after what could have been one of the most emotionally draining markets.

Having a clear and decisive intermediate to long-term *trend weighting strategy* is crucial to profitable investing.

Ben's Response:

Sometimes, profitable investing requires buying at a time when the market is the scariest and your emotions would otherwise dictate no action. The markets are always uncertain to a certain extent so it is important for a decision-maker/steward to have *a system* to trigger either a "buy-low" buying opportunity or a preserve principal, selling decision.

At Swords Wealth Management, LLC [www.swordswealthmanagement.com], we have a proprietary *trend weighting* system in place to distinguish between changes in intermediate to long-term *trends* versus short-term *noise*.

This is not the sole factor in our decision-making. This system alone has inherent weaknesses. We consider risk management on behalf of our clients too important to place sole dependency on this or any other strategy or system.

While we resist making too many short-term changes, we try to never be too stubborn to reconsider frequently all the four keys to tactical investment changes. First and foremost, we are stewards. Our goals are preservation of principal and using moneymaking growth trends for those we serve.

Financial Freedom for Owners

True financial stewards are making SMART CHOICES in STRONG TRUST based on repeatable, reasonable expectations instead of mere hope and weak trust. The best way for long-term investors to buy low and sell high may very well be to borrow the knowledge, skill, and experience of a *true financial steward* by delegating such decisions to them.

Once an owner experiences the results of these SMART CHOICES, their confidence goes up and they develop the STRONG TRUST needed for financial peace of mind. We learn to let go and enjoy the *complete* financial freedom our *true financial steward* provides.

[ii] SEE IMPORTANT ENDNOTE DISCLOSURES

>> CHAPTER 11

THE BRIDGE TO *COMPLETE* FREEDOM

But solid food is for the mature, who because of practice have their senses trained to discern good and evil.

– HEBREWS 5:14

Rich people are bigger than their problems. Poor people are smaller than their problems.

– T. HARV EKER, Secrets of the Millionaire Mind: *Mastering the Inner Game of Wealth*

>> IF WE CAN DEVELOP *HIGH FAITH* IN A PARTNER FOR OUR FINANCIAL FUTURE, WE CAN REAP PEACE OF MIND FOR A LIFETIME.

>> WITHOUT *FULL RELEASE* OF RESPONSIBILITIES TO OUR DELEGATE, THERE IS NO *COMPLETE* FREEDOM.

>> THIS IS HOW THE CODEPENDENT CYCLE OF TRUST, EXPECTATIONS (OR HOPES), FAITH ACTIONS, AND EXPERIENCE WORKS.

Steve's Story: Cross *the Bridge* of *High Faith* to *Complete* Freedom.

We sleep peacefully at night in the midst of financial storms. We have that certain settling feeling we can't quite explain. We have financial peace of mind and *complete* financial freedom. We arrived there because of *high faith* in our delegate. Our delegate has proven to be a *true financial steward*, skilled and highly responsible.

Others want *complete* financial freedom. They want to cross *the bridge* over the *chasm of concerns* to financial peace of mind. They want to fully release the concerns of the responsibilities of wealth. They need their trust to grow strong and their faith to be high in the person to whom they release these responsibilities.

DEVELOP FAITH IN THE STEWARD

We know a *true financial steward* is a person having authority. Experiencing this authority is the source of our increasing trust and financial peace of mind. We are beginning to cross over *the bridge*, over our *chasm of concerns*. Our engagement with our steward is one of faith in our delegate, our financial partner.

As owners stay engaged with them, their faith rises toward *complete* financial freedom.

If owners can develop *high faith* in a partner for our financial future, we can reap peace of mind for a lifetime.

START WITH LITTLE AND KEEP MOVING FORWARD

In order to reach peace of mind, we must start with at least a little trust. It may be borrowed trust. It may be borrowed from those of experience, those who have had their senses exercised to discern SMART CHOICES. Those mature. Those wise. Those parents. Those leaders. Those elders.

In matters of delegating and releasing wealth responsibilities, financial peace of mind could be borrowed from either speaking to existing clients of a prospective advisor or from other trusted, non-biased financial professionals such as CPAs. These are persons who have their own positive experience with the steward-advisor. Hopefully, they have "arrived." Financial peace of mind with *complete* financial freedom is a destiny.

As you borrow the trusted experiences of faith others have, you will begin to have your own personal experiences. You are moving forward little by little. Your trust grows stronger and your faith grows higher.

Trust is to faith like an anchor is to a flying kite. A kite needs an anchor. A good anchor is engaged with flying the kite. It lets the kite ride the wind. It rises higher and higher, overcoming gravity.

Faith in matters of delegating wealth management can rise up like that. It rides the changing winds in enjoyable financial peace of mind. This is what the clients of *true financial stewards* experience over time.

Our trust is in *clear, reasonable expectations.*

Our faith is in our steward being highly responsible as well as skilled.

This trust and faith is engaged.

EXPERIENCE FAITH WITH TRUST: ENGAGED

For *complete* financial freedom, we should develop *high faith*, but how do we really get there? How do we move from little to much?

We have talked about what type of person is capable of truly delivering what we need. A person who is a *true financial steward*. And we have talked about the importance of delegating in order to receive the freedom we want. But we also discussed that without *full release* of responsibilities to our delegate, there is no *complete* freedom.

We need to *fully release* wealth responsibilities in *high faith*, but how? This is easier said than done.

First, recognize there is a difference between trust and faith. To reach peace of mind is an engaging effort that involves embracing both these emotional components of our financial life.

Second, understand the difference between "blind faith" and what we call *high faith*.

We are talking about our financial peace of mind; an emotional as well as tangible reality. It involves trust, but also involves faith. While different, these two are engaged together, co-dependent. They are connected by experiences and expectations (or hope). This could be pictured as seen in Exhibit 11 -1.

Exhibit 11 -1

TRUST, NO ACTION PROBLEMS

Trust is something we are willing to act on, whether we do so or not. Trust, by itself, does not have experiences. It simply "believes." When we liken trust to mere beliefs, we are saying it can be exclusive of actions.

Experiences are the result of trust put in action. Trust engaged with action is the real definition of faith. As stated above, to a certain extent, trust and faith are engaged; they are dependent on each other.

For example, we can trust that food will nourish us, but if we only trust and do not act on that trust, if we don't actually eat, then we will not be nourished. Despite the food being real and the principal being true, we starve for lack of action.

It is possible to believe strongly, even trust strongly, and yet never take action on that trust. Trust with no action is no faith and does little, if any, good. Problems will remain.

The person who knows they should delegate certain financial responsibilities but doesn't is like the person who knows they should eat to live, but simply don't. Both experience dire results and problems continue.

WEAK TRUST, "BLIND FAITH," WORRY

Faith is when we have trust, we have a belief or conviction, and we engage it with action. By experience, we understand that if we don't want problems to continue, we must exercise some faith. We must DO something. There is an old saying, "For things to change, we've got to change."

Christians, in particular, often wonder why faith does not work sometimes and other times it does. Why do we sometimes fail to get the results we want with faith? In finances, we might wonder why we linger with financial problems and worries. Perhaps we trust in the wrong things.

If we trust in what is yet unproven, unrepeatable, and untrustworthy, we are exercising "blind faith" not *high faith*. We are acting without any real confidence. We have insufficient experience, belief, or trust. Many will throw up a prayer and act without true hope, without defining expectations.

Once again, trust is to faith like an anchor is to flying a kite. It is like trying to fly a kite in the wind without it being anchored to anything. It will spiral down eventually. Without some trust (i.e., the anchor) there can be no faith (i.e., the flying kite).

In this book we have talked about the financial cliffs. Making financial choices with WEAK TRUST is like walking near a cliff. And financial anxiousness and worry is a deep chasm. Delegating responsibility for the concerns of wealth management with WEAK TRUST and a poor release of those concerns allows financial anxiety to continue.

FROM WEAK TRUST TO STRONG TRUST & SMART CHOICES

"Blind faith" is WEAK TRUST and little, if any, real faith. Whether we like it or not, delegation of financial responsibilities to a steward will only bridge financial anxiety or other financial concerns if we can develop STRONG TRUST and *high faith* in our steward.

So where does STRONG TRUST and *high faith* come from? The key is in the engagement of expectations (trust) and actions (faith). The owner and the steward set expectations. The owner trusts the expectations and the steward does their part to fulfill expectations.

"Blind faith" is acting without accountability and with a lack of clearly defined or reasonable expectations. It is not necessarily anchored in what is proven, repeatable, or trustworthy.

So it makes sense that *high faith* is anchored with accountability and with *clear, reasonable expectations* that can be proven, repeatable or found trustworthy.

So trust and faith are engaged in taking action on *clear, reasonable expectations*.

UNDERSTAND THE CYCLE TO RISING FAITH

Taking action, exercising faith, on clear expectations creates an experience.

For example, the owner takes an action by delegating wealth management authority to the steward. The *steward's authority* paints the expectations clearly in the owner's mind. The steward takes actions according to the defined expectations.

If the owner's mind is engaged in the action based on the clear expectations, it records the experience. Trust draws on the clear expectation, its related action, and the resulting experience to create a *reasonable expectation* going forward.

Once again, *clear, reasonable expectations* are the key.

That sounds confusing. But it is really just a cycle. Please refer again to Exhibit 11-1 as I try to simplify it.

For example, for most people, the knowledge of gravity comes with very *clear, reasonable expectations.* The first time we stepped off a high curb, we experienced an unseen force, gravity. This unseen force tended to show itself over the course of our life. As an older person, now we have a set of *clear, reasonable expectations* about gravity. We have STRONG TRUST in gravity.

Every little action to test gravity reaffirmed our expectation with an experience. And we have a **set of trustworthy experiences** reinforcing our **set of reasonable expectations**. The more times we went around the reinforcing cycle of trust, expectation, faith, and experience regarding gravity, the stronger our engagement of trust and faith became.

This STRONG TRUST in gravity breeds *high faith* to make a SMART CHOICE. We STEP AWAY from the top ledge of the skyscraper. We don't need to experience the fall. Our curb experience taught us a less damaging lesson of what to expect.

High faith is in the development of higher expectations through the positive experiences of engaging trust with action. It is actually confidence to act as a result of developing stronger and stronger trust in the cycle of rising faith.

SCIENTIFIC TRUST IS NOT THE ONLY TRUST

Someone says, "I'll believe it when I see it." This person is like a scientist. They believe only in what science can prove in the sense realm, the tangible things.

However, it is possible to have expectations that draw trust into authoritative action based merely on hearsay.

Christians believe in the life, death, and resurrection of Jesus Christ despite the lack of direct experience with Jesus in the flesh. We may also not possess or know much, if any, hard evidence of Jesus's life, what some call sense-realm evidence.

Our set of expectations can be mere hope. That's okay. If that hope motivates us to take action, we are walking in faith and we have the opportunity to have personal experiences.[1]

Prior to having personal experience, we are borrowing trust. It may be borrowed from others. Those mature. Those wise. Those parents. Those leaders. Those elders. But eventually, their trust needs to become our trust if we are to be at peace in *high faith*.

---

[1] FYI: evidence does exist of Jesus Christ's life. Josh McDowell's book series on "Evidence" is a good summary of such documentary evidence. But the bigger evidence is what some call "inside information." "I was lost, but now I'm found"; a sense of new insight, new wisdom, and personal relationship with God in our soul. The "born again" inner "witness" as mentioned in Romans 8:16, "The Spirit Himself bears witness with our spirit that we are children of God...." is part of this "inside information." Others call this a "deeply personal experience." The Bible calls it a spirit to Spirit relationship. Without further debate, this "evidence," this set of experiences can breed more trust, expectations, faith and experiences leading to the *high faith* needed for true freedom.

STRONG TRUST, SMART CHOICES

Faith through all kinds of changing circumstances is where the experiences of stronger trust and confidence comes. In wealth management, our true faith anchored on trusting in *clear, reasonable expectations* earns the experience of our *steward's authority*. We enjoy the good, confidence-building experience of their dealing with changing winds.

We will move from little trust and little faith to STRONG TRUST and *high faith*.

We will cross *the bridge* to financial peace of mind by *high faith*.

Those owners who have done this, including myself, are beginning to experience *complete* financial freedom.

Start with little. Keep moving forward. Exercise faith with trust. Be engaged. Stay engaged watching expectations turn to personal experiences and growing trust. These are SMART CHOICES. You too will arrive at the *complete* financial freedom this book has promised.

Ben's Response:

Our concern and responsibilities do not end once we have concluded our meetings with our clients. Not only do we commit to *clear, reasonable expectations*, but we establish and share with them calendars for actionable items over the next several years.

This does help owners to grow trust. But frankly, owners need more than mere trust to achieve financial freedom. Owners must delegate and fully release in order to cross that bridge.

If you lack the desire, knowledge, skill, experience, or time to manage your wealth, then the SMART CHOICE is to seek someone like our practice and begin building trust and faith today.

Allow us to serve you until your faith grows and your confidence builds to the point of *full release* of wealth responsibilities.

Our process is built to give our clients a chance to develop STRONG TRUST and the courage to release worry and enjoy *complete* financial freedom.

>> CHAPTER 12

FINDING A POTENTIAL STEWARD-ADVISOR

Begin the Search

Again, the kingdom of heaven is like
a merchant seeking fine pearls,
and upon finding one pearl of great value,
he went and sold all that he had and bought it.
– MATTHEW 13:45-46

>> FIRST WE MUST DECIDE WHO WE ARE AND WHAT WE WANT

>> NOT ONLY IS CHOOSING THE RIGHT ADVISOR IMPORTANT FOR THE OWNER, BUT IT IS IMPORTANT FOR THE OWNER'S HEIRS.

>> WE WANT SOMEBODY WHO IS NOT NEBULOUS; NOT JUST "OUT THERE," NEVER SEEN, TALKED TO, OR HEARD BY THE OWNER.

Steve's Story: The Essential Step to Cross *the Bridge* of *High Faith*.

Financial lives can be emotionally torn up in the *chasm of chaos*, a chasm of financial concerns that can literally de-energize and cause even the lives of persons of wealth to spiral downward in despair.

But this does not have to be so. Financial peace of mind is in reach and *complete* financial freedom is possible. But it requires crossing *the bridge* of *high faith* to pass over the *chasm of chaos*, the chasm of financial concerns.

I have proposed that if we can develop *high faith* in a partner for our financial future, we can reap financial peace of mind for a lifetime.

Most Christians believe that choosing the right marriage partner is the first most significant decision in life after choosing to make Jesus Christ Lord of our life. At the risk of overstepping, perhaps the third most significant decision in life for people of any amount of significant wealth is the choice of a financial advisor for our personal financial planning and wealth management.

I consider it an essential step toward *complete* financial freedom. Without the right advisor, the owner will be tied up in tedious and chaotic long-term responsibilities of wealth instead of enjoying freedom. And the long-term preservation of our lifestyle and our estates could be at risk in the hands of an untested and possibly untrustworthy advisor.

I have heard it said by estate planning professionals that statistical surveys prove that accumulated wealth is lost almost entirely by the second generation after the wealth accumulator's death. That means within 40 years after someone has accumulated wealth, that wealth, if left to heirs, will be gone. Not only is choosing the right advisor important for the owner, but it is important for the owner's heirs.

HOW TO FIND A POTENTIAL STEWARD-ADVISOR

In Chapter 6 we discussed who and what we want in a financial partner for life – a *true financial steward* who can really ***deliver*** on the *steward's assurance* of financial peace of mind.

In this chapter we are focused on how to begin the search for a potential steward-advisor, someone who will potentially be one of the most valuable contributors to our household, a *true financial steward.*

Step#1: We must understand who seeks a steward-advisor and what we are seeking in a steward-advisor.

WHO SEEKS A STEWARD-ADVISOR

The promise of financial peace of mind and *complete* financial freedom from the concerns of wealth management is for people who possess the following attitudes:

- We are willing to develop stronger and stronger trust little by little in a highly responsible person.
- We are willing to follow guidance in designing and following well-defined plans with the help of a person of true *steward's authority* intent on helping us avoid the cliffs of the *chasm of financial concerns.*
- We are willing to fully release wealth responsibilities with *high faith* in a partner for our financial future as that person proves themselves to be a *true financial steward.*

WHAT WE ARE SEEKING IN A STEWARD-ADVISOR

Now that we have clarified who seeks a steward-advisor, we must understand what we are seeking in a steward-advisor in order to know where to begin our search.

In general financial planning and household wealth management, many areas of financial discipline will be involved. A person who seeks a steward-advisor is seeking a delegate who is a generalist, like the coach of a football team, rather than a specialist, like a player on that team.

Players/Specialist

Each player on a football team has a particular discipline, a position or specialty other players don't have. A defensive safety does not act the same as a nose guard. And a lineman does not act the same as a running back. The team's success is dependent upon each individual player executing their discipline.

In the financial services world, the following special financial disciplines have designated players a financial coach can call on.

Insurance, or risk management as some call it, can involve insurance agents for life insurance, property and casualty insurance, and various health-related insurable coverages. These should have expert knowledge in their insurance field.

Stockbrokers are licensed to sell investment securities. They will have expert knowledge concerning what investment securities are being offered for sale or investments and who is suitable for those securities.

Income tax practitioners such as enrolled agents or Certified Public Accountants limiting themselves primarily to tax return preparation will have expert knowledge in personal or corporate income tax and estate and trust tax laws.

In today's modern financial service offerings, it is not uncommon to see a lot of crossover in the way that those experts listed above hold themselves out to the public. Insurance agents are starting to sell securities. Stockbrokers are starting to sell insurance. CPAs also are starting to get involved in securities sales.

But keep in mind, for the most part they remain focused on their primary expertise or discipline; their position. When they are involved in the general financial planning process, their expertise in their discipline can be invaluable.

Coaches/Generalists

Like a coach on the football team, the generalist will know the function of all positions on the team and how each player's assignment contributes to each football play. They will tend to have a game plan as well as coordinate the execution of that game plan.

Certain Certified Financial Planners (CFP®) and certain ***Registered Investment Advisors*** or CPAs focused on general financial planning services will have a broad knowledge of where each financial specialty fits within the big picture of household financial and investment planning.

These are a good starting point in our search for a steward-advisor who will be qualified as a potential *true financial steward* for persons of wealth.

Step#2: Before our search begins, we must decide in general who we want.

Among the top considerations of who we want are the following:

- Someone we hope and expect we can trust
- Someone we could develop *high faith* in
- Someone who we can observe their life

First, who is somebody we hope and expect we can trust?

This brings hope into the equation. Hope is not something solidly in hand at the moment but rather is something that can be proved "little by little." We must have someone in whom we could possibly develop STRONG TRUST.

Remember, we want someone with enough *steward's authority* to help us have *clear, reasonable expectations* that can draw out our trust into smart actions. These smart choices will prove to be good experience, which fosters even stronger trust.

Think about this. This eliminates many people who have shown low integrity and little or no attitude to serve or somebody of no experience; no financial authority in their voice.

Second, who is somebody we could have *high faith* in? For me this quickly pointed to the "Christian" screen as mentioned in Chapter 6. Without a positive answer to those questions, I doubt I could ever have *high faith* in that person as my financial steward.

Third, who is somebody that we can observe their life? This is not always face-to-face anymore. It can now be through social media or through reputation and borrowing the trust in the subject of other friends or financial professionals.

Of course, we are looking for someone of skill, integrity, and quality service.

And we want somebody who is not nebulous; not just "out there," never seen, talked to, or heard by the owner.

Most investment "money managers" love to practice this way. They are only account managers. They will tell us, "My service is limited to managing your account for my fee." I have suggested that having a mere account manager may be good for some assets as a specialist, but not for your overall household financial security.

Unfortunately, even local advisors calling themselves financial planners may want to operate like account managers, treating us as merely "assets under management." Once we observe this is their manner of service, we should run the other way.

Step#3: Begin the search after deciding where to *look* and where to *meet* them.

WHERE TO *LOOK* TO FIND POSSIBLE STEWARD-ADVISORS

Essentially, defining **what** and **who** we are looking for helps us to define **where** to search.

- Where do we find somebody of sound financial knowledge, skill, and experience who is also a generalist coach instead of a specialist player? We want an expert in overall financial planning.
- Where do we find someone in whom we can expect to grow trust by observing their handling of circumstances over time?
- Where do we find someone we could develop *high faith* in? Do we want a Christian?
- Where do we find somebody who is observable? Where we can hear their voice and experience their *steward's authority*?

Our ability to grow STRONG TRUST and ***release*** responsibility to these generalists was discussed in Chapter 6, where we defined a financial steward and discussed the "Christian" screen and the interview and trial period for testing such stewards.

WHERE TO MEET THEM

If the *who* we are after is a Christian, we could start by...

- **...looking in local churches or Christian fellowships**. Ask the elders or ministers, "Who do you know that works with financial planning and investments that is a person of knowledge, integrity, and service?"

While we may not necessarily have to meet someone face to face, it is essential that we hear the authority in their voice. A person of true knowledge, skill, and experience will possess financial authority.

- Although this is not a guarantee they have *steward's authority*, **a telephone screening call** to *hear* them is a good first step.

Steward-advisors may be able to be found on their website.

- Once again, with modern technology it may be possible to *hear* financial authority **in video or audio clips or through social media postings**.

We would be looking for someone who understands the importance of trust or integrity in service. Sometimes the **words in their advertisements** will allude to quality service, trust, or experience.

- Financial advisors who are generalists may be found in the **telephone book or online advertising (i.e., Yellow Pages).**

Many times financial advisors who are *true financial stewards* for a group of clients will have **events that prospective clients may attend**. If we can, we should attend these with friends who use the advisor themselves. This gives us an opportunity to hear about their trust.

- These are not necessarily financial seminars, but rather more **social events**.
- This is a good opportunity to *hear* our prospective steward without our commitment.

Ben's Response:

In Chapter 6, I wrote about where to find questions to ask a prospective financial advisor. To actually begin the process of searching for a steward-advisor, I suggest going to the website at www.CFP.net and clicking on the "Find a CFP® Professional" banner in the upper right hand corner of the page.

From here you can enter in your zip code to locate a potential advisor in your locale. Once you have selected your zip code, I encourage you to select "Refine your search" and then "Advanced search." Here you can select anything from "General Financial Planning" to more specialized disciplines like "Investment Planning" and "Estate Planning," to name just a few. This advanced search feature will help you hone in on the **what** you need in terms of knowledge, skills and experience in your important quest for a steward-advisor.

It is important to note that not all CFP®s actually provide general financial planning services as a steward-advisor, which we recommend for those seeking *complete* financial freedom.

>> CHAPTER 13

FIRE THE FRAUD! HIRE THE HERO.

Now He was also saying to the disciples,
"There was a rich man who had a manager,
and this manager was reported to him
as squandering his possessions.
And he called him and said to him,
'What is this I hear about you?
Give an accounting of your management,
for you can no longer be manager.'"
– LUKE 16:1-8

>> WORLDLY ADVISORS, THOSE WHO ACT "SHREWD IN RELATION TO THEIR OWN KIND," ARE NOT THE ONES WE SHOULD USE AS WEALTH MANAGERS.

>> ...MANY WEALTH MANAGERS SHOULD BE FIRED.

>> TRUE CHRISTIAN ADVISORS WILL HAVE A CONSCIENCE THAT WILL NOT ALLOW THEM TO DEFRAUD THE OWNER.

>> IF THEY PROVE TO BE *TRUE FINANCIAL STEWARDS* ...THEY ARE THE TRUE HEROES.

Steve's Story: Fire the fraud! Hire the hero.

If a true financial steward is worthy of management, wouldn't it be true that many wealth managers should be fired?

A Bible story tells of a manager who is reported as squandering the owner's assets. The owner had not been reviewing reports very regularly, apparently having extended "blind faith" to the wealth manager.

When the owner asked the wealth manager to "give an accounting," the manager acted even more selfish, though shrewd in the eyes of the world, in utterly defrauding the owner. Speaking with many of the investment partners of the owner, he negotiated great financial favor for them at the expense of the very owner he served. (Luke 16:1-8)

What are we to make of this?

Worldly advisors, those who act "shrewd in relation to their own kind," are not the ones we should use as wealth managers.

STEWARDS OF CONSCIENCE

Ultimately, each advisor must be tested, and held accountable for his own actions. True Christian advisors will have a conscience that will not allow them to defraud the owner.

These are those who work "as unto the Lord." They are governed by more than just the fee that is paid to them. They recognize a day coming in which they will have to give an account of deeds done in their life. They want to do their best to always maintain a blameless conscience before God and before men. (Acts 24:15-16; Matthew 16:26-27)

FIRE THE FRAUD

Many times in Scripture Jesus Christ tells parables. These are made-up stories to illustrate a point. However, in Luke 16 Jesus is telling of an actual historical account in which "a certain rich man" had a steward.

Because of the inappropriate actions with the rich man's wealth, the rich man concluded he would put him out of the stewardship. "You can no longer be steward." "You can no longer be manager." "You can't be my manager any longer." These are different Bible translations saying the same thing: "Fire the fraud."

HIRE THE HERO

Highly responsible servants are available to manage and preserve wealth. People of any amount of significant wealth should move that wealth to advisors of good conscience. Owners should interview and hire these advisors under a testing period. If they prove to be *true financial stewards* who preserve wealth for the owner, the owner's heirs and for the kingdom, they are the true heroes.

Seriously consider a practice like that of Swords Wealth Management, LLC (www.swordswealthmanagement.com) to be your partner in providing you with financial peace of mind for a lifetime and *complete* financial freedom.

>> CHAPTER 14

CONCLUSIONS

>> WE CAN GET AWAY FROM "BLIND FAITH" WHICH HIRES THE WRONG ADVISOR, ONE WHO CANNOT OFFER THE *STEWARD'S ASSURANCE.*

>> HIGHLY RESPONSIBLE FINANCIAL ADVISORS WHO HAVE THE ATTITUDE OF STEWARDS ARE AVAILABLE.

>> THIS PARTNERSHIP WILL HELP US CROSS *THE BRIDGE* TO FINANCIAL PEACE OF MIND AND *COMPLETE* FINANCIAL FREEDOM.

Steve's Conclusions:

Highly responsible advisors who have the attitude of stewards are available. Advisors who hold themselves out as steward-advisors doing broad-based financial and investment planning are worth seeking out as potential *true financial stewards.*

Just as Ben Dean is doing with my wife and me, these steward-advisors can help us develop our own peace of mind definition and walk with us as we achieve it.

They help us STEP BACK and STEP AROUND the cliffs that can devastate us financially: spending based on poor lifestyle estimates, quick and poor decisions, and poor delegation.

We can get away from "blind faith" which hires the wrong advisor, one who cannot offer the *steward's assurance* or help us fully release our financial worries.

With a clear course for screening and hiring a *true financial steward*, we can engage and begin developing STRONG TRUST with solid financial and investment plans based on *clear, reasonable expectations.*

These are the essentials of *high faith* that help us truly enjoy our retirement years. This partnership will help us cross *the bridge* to financial peace of mind and *complete* financial freedom.

Delegate Now

If you lack the desire, knowledge, skill, or experience to handle your own long-term personal financial plans and investment planning, you should delegate that responsibility to someone worthy of *high faith*.

I know that trust is quantifiable; that *true financial stewards* are accountable; and that peace of mind is obtainable.

Delegating to a *true financial steward* is the real path to...

- ...Confidence,
- ...Security,
- ...Financial peace of mind, and
- ...*Complete* financial freedom.

Ben's Response:

We express to our clients that Swords Wealth Management, LLC wants to be the last financial advisor that they will ever need. This is because we view our role as *true financial stewards* to ***deliver*** the *steward's assurance* throughout their financial lives; to guide, decide, or coach them through SMART CHOICES toward *complete* financial freedom.

Isn't this what you really want in an advisor?

i & ii. IMPORTANT DISCLOSURE INFORMATION

Swords Wealth Management, LLC ("SWM") is registered as an investment adviser with the state of Texas and only transacts business in states where it is properly registered, or is excluded or exempted from registration requirements. Registration as an investment adviser does not constitute an endorsement of the firm by securities regulators nor does it indicate that the adviser has attained a particular level of skill or ability.

This book is a publication of Steve A. Swords with Benjamin H. Dean. They are advisors of Swords Wealth Management LLC. Information presented is believed to be factual and up-to-date, but we do not guarantee its accuracy and it should not be regarded as a complete analysis of the subjects discussed. All expressions of opinion reflect the judgment of the authors as of the date of publication and are subject to change. Due to various factors, including changing market conditions, discussions in this book may no longer be reflective of SWM's current expressions of opinions. Moreover, no client or prospective client should assume that any such discussion serves as the receipt of, or a substitute for, personalized advice from SWM or from any other investment professional. Moreover, any reference to persons in our book are not to be considered as a testimonial from any present or past client.

The images used in this book are from stock photos and are not clients of SWM.

Information on this book does not involve the rendering of personalized investment advice, but is limited to the dissemination of general information on products and services. A professional adviser should be consulted before implementing any of the strategies presented. Content should not be viewed as an offer to buy or sell, or a solicitation of any offer to buy or sell the securities mentioned herein. No portion of the content serves as the receipt of personalized advice from SWM or from any other investment professional. To the extent that a reader has any questions regarding the applicability of any content to his/her individual situation, he/she is encouraged to consult with the professional advisors of his/her choosing. For information pertaining to the registration status of SWM, please contact the Texas State Securities Board. A copy of SWM's current written disclosure statement discussing SWM business operations, services, and fees is available from SWM upon written request or from our website www.SwordsWealthManagement.com. SWM does not make any representations or warranties as to the accuracy, timeliness, suitability, completeness, or relevance of any information prepared by any unaffiliated third party, whether linked to the SWM web site or incorporated herein, and takes no responsibility therefore. All such information is provided solely for convenience purposes only and all users thereof should be guided accordingly.

Please remember that past performance may not be indicative of future results. Different types of investments involve varying degrees of risk, and there can be no assurance that the future performance of any specific investment or investment strategy (including those undertaken or recommended by SWM) will be profitable or equal any historical performance level(s).

Each client and prospective client agrees, as a condition precedent to his/her/its access to this book, to release and hold harmless SWM, its officers, directors, owners, employees and agents from any and all adverse consequences resulting from any of his/her/its actions and/or omissions which are independent of his/her/its receipt of personalized individual advice from SWM.

Investing strategies, such as asset allocation, diversification, rebalancing, or trend weighting, do not assure or guarantee better performance and cannot eliminate the risk of investment losses. There are no guarantees that a portfolio employing these or any other strategy will outperform a portfolio that does not engage in such strategies.

For more information including
Swords Wealth Management LLC's Form ADV
please visit

www.SwordsWealthManagement.com
or call 903-526-MONY [6669]

Made in United States
Orlando, FL
04 November 2026

90205153R00120